The Liberated Dog

The Liberated Dog

Matthew Margolis

with
Julie Grayson

HOLT, RINEHART and WINSTON
NEW YORK

Copyright © 1977 by Matthew Margolis

All rights reserved, including the right to reproduce this book or portions thereof in any form.
Published simultaneously in Canada by Holt, Rinehart and Winston of Canada, Limited.

Library of Congress Cataloging in Publication Data

Margolis, Matthew.
  The liberated dog.
  Includes index.
  1. Dogs—Training. 2. Dog breeds. I. Grayson, Julie, joint author. II. Title.
SF431.M43   636.7'08'3   76-29909
ISBN 0-03-014061-7

First Edition

Designer: Kathy Peck

Photographs by Nancy Strouss and George Bargad.

Printed in the United States of America
10 9 8 7 6 5 4 3 2 1

To Ralph Ricci,
whose concern and involvement
made this book a reality.

Acknowledgments

I am grateful to Carlos Mejias, one of the finest dog trainers I have ever known; to Kathy Mills, Bob Stern, Cindy Sikora, and Tom Shelby, for their involvement; to Nancy and Jason Strouss, for her photographic ability and his photogenic qualities; and special thanks to my editor, Don Hutter, without whose patience and fantastic editorial ability this book might never have been.

CONTENTS

Foreword

AMERICANS are acquiring dogs as never before. Today some forty million families own dogs. A dog in the house has become as much a part of the American scene as the take-out meal or the tie-dyed T-shirt.

The reasons for wanting a dog are as varied as the assortment of available breeds and mutts. Out in the suburbs, young parents want a dog "for the children." In the city, young couples want a dog "because we have no children." A working person living alone seeks companionship when he or she arrives home. A middle-aged matron wants some being to care for, and an elderly widower longs for a devoted friend. Some people feel they need protection, others hope to achieve status, and many more simply love dogs!

So now you, the city dweller, or you, the suburban or country homeowner, leap onto the bandwagon and purchase a dog. Your new pet becomes a key member of the family, and you take him along on your many excursions away from home. He springs into the car with you for a visit to family or friends. He joins you for an outing in the park or at the beach. He accompanies you through a procession of shops.

If, like many Americans, mobility has become part of your life-style, if you are spending more and more leisure time away from home, your dog will have to be mobile, too. It will be essential, therefore, that he know how to behave both in and out of your home, that he understand the basic obedience commands in any and all situations, and, what has become increasingly important, that he be trained "off leash."

This book is addressed to these modern needs. At the National Institute of Dog Training, I have trained over ten thousand dogs. Based on this experience, *The Liberated Dog* sets forth a three-part training program: (1) solutions to common behavioral problems, (2) basic obedience training, and (3) off-leash training. It applies to the new puppy as well as to the mature dog. It is a complete training curriculum.

A fundamental of my philosophy of dog training is that the *owner* teach the dog. With this book, you will learn how to communicate with your dog, how to make him understand what it is you want him to do. You will learn that the best place to train your dog is in your home. And you will learn how to carry out his training with a combination of firmness, patience, and love.

Each area of training is handled in a unique way. We start off by taking a new approach to behavioral problems. Housebreaking, barking, chewing, digging up the yard, etc., are discussed within the framework of the environment in which you live. Some problems arise more frequently with dogs that live in the suburbs; others apply more to city dogs. You will learn what causes these different behavioral problems, how you can anticipate and avoid them, and finally what you—the city or suburban owner—can do to overcome them.

The next section takes up basic obedience training. Here, you will learn how to teach your dog all the on-leash commands. And while you are teaching your dog how to "Heel," "Sit," "Stay," etc., you will be receiving additional instruction on how to apply such commands to any remaining behavioral problems.

Once your dog graduates from this basic training course, he will be ready to move on to more advanced training, to a postgraduate course in "off leash." Which brings us to the special point of this book.

With *The Liberated Dog* we take a giant step forward in the literature of dog training. This is the first book to offer an off-leash training program, moreover one specifically geared to the needs and capacities of the average dog owner.

The professional cost of training a dog off leash runs between $500 and $1,000! Now you—the average dog owner—can conduct your own off-leash training program. Your expenditure, depending on the dog, is a half hour to an hour a day, and the price of this book.

As its name implies, off-leash training consists of teaching your dog to obey you without a leash between you. Do you have opportunities to let your dog run free, but are worried about keeping him under control? No matter. A dog trained off leash responds, instantly and absolutely, when you tell him to "Come!" Are other people, animals, or noises in the area liable to distract him? No matter. He reacts, immediately and infallibly, to your "Down!" or "Sit!" or "Stay!" This is the ultimate in dog training!

The final part of the book is a glossary of breeds. It,

too, has several distinct features. It lists the temperament and characteristics of eighty-eight breeds; it stresses the relative ease or difficulty with which each breed can be trained off leash; and it discusses each breed in terms of its ability to adjust to city or country life.

Once your dog completes this training program, you can detach him from his leash with full confidence. You will be assured of your ability to control his actions at all times, thereby guaranteeing his good behavior and safety as well as your own peace of mind. You will enjoy taking him with you wherever you go.

As for the dog, he will relish his new opportunities and revel in his new freedom to move about, to romp through a city park or race across a suburban lawn. He will be free to catch a Frisbee or gambol near children at play. In keeping with the spirit of the times, he will become . . . a liberated dog.

1

Fundamentals of Training

1

Of Dogs and Dog Training

LET US ASSUME you have just purchased a puppy. You are filled with eager spirits and rosy dreams. Images of Norman Rockwell's *Saturday Evening Post* covers dance through your head. You envision your dog fetching your slippers and dropping them at your feet, or gazing at you with adoration as you relax in your favorite morris chair. . . .

Stop right there. From the moment your puppy crosses the welcome mat into your city apartment or suburban home, reality sets in. Instead of fetching your slippers, he sniffs them and decides they smell good enough to eat. Instead of settling contentedly at your feet while you ease yourself into your chair, he beats you to it and claims the seat for himself. Your dog's behavior dismays you. He snatches the sirloin from the dining-room table, he chews the curtains behind the living-room couch. He leaps into your lap, disregarding the cup of hot coffee you hold in your hand. He uses your satin bedspread as his private trampoline.

3

What do you do? Give vent to your annoyance and scold him? Smack him? Lock him in a dark closet?

Does punishment work?

Let's look in on a dog owner who tries it. His pet Hilda remains alone in his city apartment all day. When he gets home from work, Hilda leaps into the air and greets him in a frenzy of unrestrained joy. He is all smiles, until he surveys the living room and spots a damp area in the middle of the rug. The phone rings and a neighbor complains that the dog has been barking all day. Deep furrows appear between his eyebrows. He strides into the bedroom and spots the chewed-up strings in his tennis racket. In a rage, he picks up the tattered racket and hurls it at the dog.

Hilda flees to the safety of the kitchen. She cowers beneath the table, ears drooping, tail hanging low. She has no idea what went wrong. . . .

Another dog owner resorts to a different form of punishment. The lady of a surburban house lets Harry, the new family dog, out into the backyard. At three o'clock the children arrive home from school and the dog trails them back into the house.

Moments later, Harry's mistress walks into the kitchen and sees the children playing with their new pet. A fond maternal smile crosses her face: companionship for the children, this is what having a dog is all about! But then she glances out the window . . . and sees her prize begonias trampled to the ground. She turns to the living room and catches sight of the soil and brambles Harry has tracked onto the oriental rug. Shouting, "You bad, bad dog!" she lifts Harry by the scruff of the neck and tosses him out the side door.

Harry lands lightly on the grass, but gazes sadly back at the house. What did he do wrong?

Punishment succeeds only in convincing your dog

that you are angry with him; it doesn't teach him how you want him to behave. Obviously it is not the answer; *training* your dog is.

Training is the only way for a dog and his owner to live in harmony. Every dog wants to please his master, but an untrained dog doesn't know how. Confused and saddened by his master's repeated disapproval and anger, he grows fearful, then either hostile or shy. Meanwhile you, the owner, are more and more irritated by your dog's unruly behavior, more and more puzzled by his refusal to obey. You are driven to screaming, slapping, or worse!

But the situation is not hopeless; it is more like a faulty connection in the lines of communication between you and your dog.

A frequent misconception among dog owners is that their pet is really a four-legged human being. They credit him with human ability to think and to plan, even to plot. "Max is so smart," they may say. "Every time he does something wrong he runs under the couch and hides." Or, "Minnie is so spiteful. Whenever I go out, she purposely chews on the carpet."

Let's face it, your dog's capacity for reasoning or abstract thinking is nil. If Max hides when you enter the room it is because he has learned to associate your arrival with some sort of punishment. And if Minnie goes on a chewing rampage, it is usually out of normal puppiness, sometimes out of a sense of anxiety or frustration, but not because she is trying to teach you a lesson.

Since you cannot reach your dog through reasoning or by instilling fear, how, then, do you train him? It is necessary, first, to understand him.

A dog is a creature who needs love. While he may react with terror to punishment, he responds with total joy to affection and approval. He thrives on a kind word, a gentle pat, on any attention from his master. Stroking his back or tossing him a stick to catch are as necessary to his well-being as is his daily ration of food.

His primary desire is to please you. It's in his makeup, he is genetically conditioned to give obedience and loyalty to his master. If he understands how you want him to behave, if he is aware of what meets with your approval, if he knows what it is he may and may not do, he will make every effort to act accordingly.

But you wonder, how does he *learn* what pleases you? Which leads to the next point.

A dog learns by association. As every schoolchild knows, it was the sound of a bell that triggered the appetite of Pavlov's dog. If your dog's action elicits a "positive" response (love and approval), he will associate that response with his action, and he will be eager to repeat it.

Armed with this knowledge of your dog—his need for love and affection, his desire to please, and his ability to learn through positive association—you are ready to learn the proper means and methods of training him.

The best place to train your dog is in your own home or apartment.

You can always board your dog at a training school to undergo an obedience course for several weeks. If the course succeeds, your dog arrives home trained to obey the trainer. He is familiar with the trainer's commands, the trainer's gestures, the trainer's tone of voice. But does he understand that he is supposed to obey *you*?

He may be adjusted to a housebreaking schedule and educated in all the obedience commands, and he may respond when you tell him to "Sit" or to "Stay." But the training school cannot duplicate the home environment. What about all the behavior problems that arise in the house? Does he know that he mustn't run out the front door when you answer the bell? Does he understand that the garbage pail is off limits? Is he aware that he mustn't use the sofa for his afternoon nap?

Since all your dog's problems arise in the home, what better place is there to train him? Since the dog must learn how *you* want him to behave, it is essential that *you* do the training.

Punishment is not training. The proper training procedure is correction and praise.

When your dog misbehaves, do not punish him; that's "negative." As we have just seen, punishing or instilling fear in your dog only serves to confuse him and may, eventually, warp his personality. Punishment does not teach your dog how to behave.

So you are going to learn a "positive" method; you are going to "correct" him. The "correction" encourages your dog to stop whatever he is doing wrong. Immediately following the "correction," you must speak right up and lavish him with praise. Tell him how smart he is, belt out an enthusiastic "Good dog!" and pat him lovingly.

Your dog now makes a "positive" association; he learns that *stopping* this behavior is what pleases you. There is no need to bribe him with special treats or an extra helping of meat. You merely let him know how wonderful he is for obeying you.

Training requires a consistent attitude. This is fundamental. You must set down certain rules of behavior for your pet and you must enforce these rules one hundred percent of the time. You cannot allow any exceptions.

You must not feed him from the table "just this once" if you want him to learn that "Dinner is served" means his bowl of food on the floor. You must not allow him to jump up on you when you are wearing jeans if you do not want him to jump up on you when you are black-tied or gowned.

Approving his behavior some of the time and prohibiting the very same behavior at other times is confusing to your dog. More important, it defeats the entire training process.

The technique of correction and praise and a consistent attitude on your part—of firmness and affection—are important in every area of training. They are essential to teaching both the basic and the off-leash commands.

It will take time and repetition for your dog to complete his training. It will require patience, a sense of purpose, and a willingness to work with your dog. It isn't easy, but the reward will be up to fifteen years of love and companionship with an obedient and happy pet.

WHEN TO START HIS TRAINING

At seven weeks of age, a puppy is ready to be weaned from his mother and make the transition to a human master. This is also the time to start training.

From seven weeks to sixteen weeks is the most crucial period in the social development of a dog. It is during this time that his personality takes form, that he forges his basic relationship with human beings.

If you do not know how to handle his behavioral problems during this period, if you give in to anger or annoyance, your puppy will develop permanent scars on his personality.

At twelve weeks of age, after the puppy has had all his shots, you may begin housebreaking training for most breeds. Also at twelve weeks, the puppy is sufficiently mature to start on the basic obedience commands.

Many owners never think about "school days" for dogs until their pets are six months or older. Why do they wait so long? Sometimes it is a case of hope springing eternal. "My dog only has an occasional accident on the carpet, and eventually he's going to . . ." Or owners blame themselves: "My dog only chews my shoes when I leave them on the floor where she can get at them. . . ." Or they count their blessings: "It's true that my dog strews garbage all over the floor, but at least he doesn't bark all day, like the dog down the hall. . . ."

You cannot alter a dog's personality once he's past puppyhood. You can, however, train most dogs to overcome bad habits at any age.

2

Training Tools
and
Techniques

THE TOOLS you need to train your dog are few and inexpensive—simple, standard items available in most supermarkets or pet-supply stores.

The first two—the six-foot leash and the corrective collar—are the indispensable tools of dog training. Together they are used to perform the technique known as the corrective jerk, the cornerstone of all obedience training. The corrective jerk is of prime importance in overcoming stubborn puppy problems, is used to teach your dog the basic commands, and is absolutely essential to both on- and off-leash training. It will be described in detail in the following chapter.

A Six-Foot Leash

The standard leash is roughly five-eighths of an inch wide. You may, however, choose a narrower or wider one, depending on the size of your dog. A half-inch width is adequate for Toy or other small breeds, while the extra strength and weight of a three-quarter-inch width works better for large dogs.

A canvas leash is less expensive than leather and is acceptable for this training program. But bear in mind that leather is more durable and is easier on your hands.

A Corrective Collar

This kind of dog collar consists of a short length of metal links with rings at both ends. The chain is

Figure 1. Basic equipment (clockwise, from top left): long and short fishline, clothesline, six-foot leash, throw chain, choke collar, shake can.

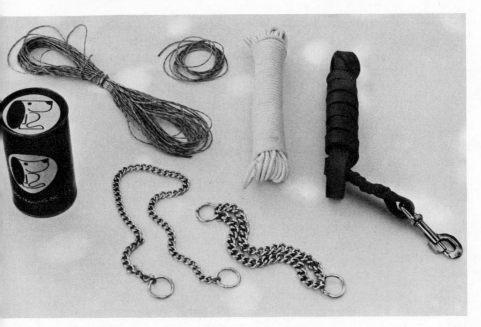

doubled back through either of the rings to form a loop that fits loosely over the dog's neck.

The links should be small, smooth, and closely forged. Linked metal makes the most effective collar and is recommended for most dogs. The metal is strong and, because of its smoothness, slides easily around the dog's neck. Linked metal is not recommended, however, for two classes of dogs. First, the very small dog is usually too fragile to withstand the weight; a collar made of lightweight nylon is better for the smaller breeds. Second, the long-coated dog—as it slides across the dog's neck the metal will catch his fur and may gradually wear it away; substitute a sturdy leather choke collar.

A SHAKE CAN

This is a do-it-yourself product. Take an empty soup or soda can and fill it part way with whatever small, metallic objects—nails, old studs or cufflinks, spare pennies—are lying around the house. Seal the top with tape.

When you shake the taped-up can, the metal objects inside produce a fierce noise, catching your dog's immediate attention. Combined with a firm "No!" it is an effective means of stopping him in the act of misbehaving.

The shake can is used primarily in overcoming a variety of puppy problems such as jumping on furniture, going into garbage, etc. It is also a tool in off-leash training.

You should keep the can out of the dog's view. If he sees you holding the can, he may anticipate its use. This will interfere with what you are trying to accomplish, which is to catch him by surprise.

The temperament of your dog will determine how

vigorously you shake the can. If your dog is placid or sedate, give the can just one quick, firm shake. If he tends to be stubborn or aggressive, it will be necessary to shake the can repeatedly with full force to produce results. And if your dog is shy or nervous, do not use the can at all. The jangling noise may frighten him. For this dog, a "No" delivered in a kindly but firm voice will be all the correction necessary.

A Throw Chain

This is cousin to the shake can. It can be any medium-weight chain of linked metal. Six inches is a good length. When tossed onto a hard floor, the clanging report startles the dog.

The throw chain is used in solving household puppy problems. It is also an important tool in off-leash training.

Do not throw the chain *at* your dog; aim it at the floor alongside him. And do not allow your pet to see you throw the chain. As with the throw can, you want the noise to take him by surprise.

A Clothesline

The line should be ten to fifteen feet long. With one end tied to the dog's collar, it acts as a long leash and allows you to administer the corrective jerk from a distance.

This becomes necessary when the shake can and the throw chain fail to solve your puppy's household problems. With the clothesline, you have long-range physical control over your dog. When he misbehaves, you are able to deliver a correction across the full length of a room.

A longer clothesline, fifty feet, is used in the intermediary stages of off-leash training.

A FISHLINE

The fishline (fifty-pound test minimum) replaces the clothesline in correcting your puppy's problems at longer distances and outdoors. The fishline is almost weightless, therefore easier to manage at distances up to one hundred feet. It is also hard to see, which together with its lack of weight gives your dog the illusion of freedom from any leash restraint, an invaluable advantage in off-leash training. When using a fishline to perform a long-range correction, you should wear a pair of sturdy gloves to keep the line from cutting into your skin.

3

THE CORRECTIVE JERK

THE CORRECTIVE JERK is the fundamental technique of dog training. It "corrects" your dog by means of a jerk applied firmly and properly on his leash. It is the easiest and fastest means of communicating to your dog how you want him to perform, it represents the most humane approach in teaching him what he may and may not do, and it sets up permanent associations in the dog's mind that lead to enduring results.

THE CORRECTIVE JERK TECHNIQUE

1. Slip a corrective collar over your dog's neck and attach a six-foot leash to the outer ring. Place your right thumb through the loop at the other end of the leash. Stand facing the same direction as your dog, on his right side.
2. With your left hand take the middle of the leash, bring it up and over to the right, and wrap it

around your right thumb, on top of the end loop. You are now holding roughly half of the leash in your right hand. The other half should dangle loosely in front of you, from your right hand to the dog's collar.

3. Clench your right hand in an upturned fist, then close your left hand over the leash right next to it, with the fist turned downward. Slip your left index finger around the pinky of your right hand so that your left hand won't slip down. If you have done this correctly, your hands will be interlocked, with your fists closed in opposite directions. This two-fisted grasp on the leash gives you firm control.

In performing a correction, jerk the leash quickly and sharply to the right. This causes a momentary tightening of the dog's collar. It serves to startle him and make him aware of your displeasure. The leash must be jerked at the very moment your dog falters in carrying out your command. In that way he associates your disapproval with his failure to perform.

It is important to jerk the leash with the proper degree of firmness. Too mild a tug produces no results. Too hard or long a jerk may frighten the dog. Do not pull him forward, yank him backward, or sweep him off his feet. Your objective is simply to startle the dog and stop his misbehavior.

In the instant you jerk the leash, call out in a no-nonsense tone "No!" Do not let anger creep into your voice—what you are aiming for is firmness, authority, and control. The dog associates the jerk with the "No," and eventually you will be able to retire the choke collar and rely on the word alone. Remember, the corrective jerk is used during the training period. It is not meant to be a permanent method of control.

The moment your dog stops his disobedience, shift the gears of your voice from firmness and authority to tones that express praise. "What a ter-

Figures 2, 3. The corrective jerk: Trainer is on right side of dog and facing in the same direction, with leash doubled up and held in both hands, which are interlocked with strap around upper thumb; jerk the leash quickly and sharply up and to the right, just enough to startle the dog.

rific dog you are! How good of you to walk by my side!" This phase of the procedure is absolutely essential. Correcting your dog is of no value unless you praise him for doing what is right.

The dog's age, size, and temperament are factors in determining the force of your correction. A small and sensitive puppy will respond to a milder correction. An older dog with the temperament of a rhinoceros will require all the full-bodied firmness you can muster.

That first jerk may produce any of several reactions. A sensitive or shy dog may start to tremble. Obviously he is frightened, and that's your cue to soften your tone or touch the next time you have to correct him. At the other end of the scale is the aggressive dog who fights the leash in an effort to get you to stop. Do not, in such cases, be intimidated. Maintain an attitude of calm, consistent control and continue to perform the corrective jerk with the same degree of firmness.

Owners are not immune to emotional reactions of their own when attempting to execute the corrective jerk for the first time. Occasionally an owner seizes upon this technique with a now-I've-got-you attitude. Needless to say, that's out. The corrective jerk is not a call to arms. Nor is it an outlet for your frustrations. If you had a grueling session with your tax accountant, or tried on eight suits and none of them fitted, forget about training for that day. Wait until you are feeling calm and rational and fair.

More often, however, owners are reluctant to use the correction. The dog will be hurt; the dog will be frightened; the dog won't like them anymore. They frequently stand there holding the leash uncertainly, hesitant about executing the jerk. That's okay. There's no harm in starting out gently. The correction may not be effective, but it will serve to reassure

18

the owner that a pull on the leash is not equivalent to pulling the switch on the electric chair.

The first time you try the technique your hands may be unsteady and the firm tug you planned to execute may come off as a niggling little nip. Don't try to make up for it by practicing on the dog, delivering a series of rapid-fire, ineffective jerks (instead, you can practice on someone's arm, or a banister). These repeated pulls are not only irritating to the dog; they will confuse him. For him to associate the correction with his misbehavior, the jerk must come at the moment he misbehaves. If you continue to tug at his leash, he will understand that you are annoyed with him but nothing else. Wait for another occasion to correct him. Then, administer the jerk with as much firmness and authority as you can muster. Do it quickly, and simultaneously tell him "No." In time, your confidence will grow, your hand will become steadier, your performance more polished.

When you correct your dog in the street, be prepared for pedestrians to stop and complain. I am frequently outdoors in my training sessions, teaching a dog to heel or training him not to run into the road. Occasionally a passerby, usually a little old lady, stops and aims her shopping bag at me. "Young man," she says, "how would you like me to do that to your neck?" She is well meaning, no doubt an animal lover, but she doesn't understand what is in the best interests of the dog. Don't let these sidewalk analysts intimidate you. If you correct your dog when he tries to dash across the street, you may be saving his life; if you correct him when he pulls ahead of you on the leash, your daily outings will become more enjoyable for both of you. It is the dog's well-being and safety that are involved. So ignore the jeers, pay no attention to the criticisms, and concentrate on training your dog!

II

Behavioral Problems

4

INTRODUCTION

LIVING SUCCESSFULLY with your new puppy depends on teaching him how to behave. You must housebreak him. You must teach him not to chew up the furniture or strew garbage over the floor. In the city, you must stop him from jumping on other passengers in the elevator; in the country, you must prevent him from digging up your lawn.

Sometimes the owner inadvertently creates a problem. Perhaps you confine your dog to one room when you leave the house. That's all right, but if it's a small area and you close the door on him, that's wrong. Being cooped up frightens your dog and makes him anxious. In his frustrated state, he may start to bark or to chew.

Instead of closing the door, buy a puppy or baby gate and set it up in the doorway. With the door open and the gate attached, your puppy is able to see into the other rooms and feels less confined. You can purchase a puppy gate in a hardware or department store. Be certain to buy one made of mesh. Avoid the accordion kind; the puppy may slip through the slats or, worse, get himself caught between them.

Some problems may be avoided by an understanding of the puppy and his needs. In this chapter I discuss why a puppy turns to such behavior as excessive barking, jumping, etc., and describe what you can do to prevent the development of these bad habits. The method you employ depends largely on the temperament of your dog.

If you are dealing with a shy or sensitive dog, do not use the shake can. The sudden clatter will frighten him. You may succeed in correcting his misbehavior, but you may at the same time turn him into a neurotic dog. Instead, correct him verbally with a firm "No." He may be sensitive enough to respond to the stern tone of your voice, and that could be all the correction he needs.

If, however, your dog is blessed with a relaxed, easygoing temperament, you may use the can with impunity. The combination of the sharp noise accompanied by your firm "No" works effectively in teaching him what he may and may not do.

And finally, if your dog is a rebel at heart, the shake can may not be enough. He may ignore the sound of the can and pay no attention to your disapproving "No." For such a dog, get out the leash and collar and use the corrective jerk.

Once you establish the proper method for correcting your dog, stay with it. Use it with firmness and consistency. It may take time, but the results will prove worthwhile.

EXERCISE

A dog is less likely to have behavioral problems if he is sound and healthy, and regular exercise is essential to such fitness for nearly all breeds. Exercise strengthens a dog's body and releases tensions. With adequate exercise, he will be more agile and alert, and more amenable to both behavioral and obedience training.

Part V in this book defines the amount and kind of exercise the different breeds require. Check your breed and read the description carefully. In general, the Toy or smaller breeds require a minimum of exercise. Several short, brisk walks a day will serve to send the blood coursing through a small dog's veins.

Most other dogs, however, require one or more vigorous workouts every day. Your dog needs to run and jump, to fetch and retrieve. He needs the excitement of interaction with you. Walk your dog to an enclosed area—a schoolyard or park is fine—and remove his leash. Spend at least half an hour in energetic play. Toss a ball and have him retrieve it. Run around the area and let him chase you.

In the country, your dog may get his daily workouts on your own property. If you don't have an enclosed yard, use a tie-out stake, available from your local pet shop.

Or you may take advantage of the trees on your property and set up an exercise run. Most hardware stores carry inexpensive cable runs. Select two trees at least twenty-five feet apart and follow the directions for installation; or simply tie a clothesline between the trees, attach a pulley to the line, and clamp this onto the dog's leash. To exercise the dog, stand at one end of the run or line and throw a ball toward the other end. Your dog will shuttle back and forth between the trees, working off his store of physical energy and enjoying a game at the same time.

5

Paper - Training and Housebreaking

Every owner faces the task of "toilet training" his new puppy. It is up to you to teach your dog that urination and defecation take place in an area that you designate and at times convenient to you.

There are two approaches to your dog's elimination needs. One is housebreaking; the other is paper-training. Housebreaking means teaching him to eliminate outdoors; paper-training is teaching him to eliminate on paper in one specific area of your house.

Contrary to popular opinion, when you paper-train a dog you do not switch to housebreaking later. Paper-training is an alternate method of handling your dog's elimination. Paper-training is forever. It is a workable solution if you own a Chihuahua or a Maltese or any puppy that will grow up to tip the scales at no more than twenty pounds.

Paper-Training

If your dog falls into this lightweight category and you opt for the newspaper, you have one immediate advantage. Because the procedure takes place indoors, you may begin his training on the day he enters your house.

Select a small, enclosed, uncarpeted area—the kitchen, bathroom, or a vinyl-tiled den is fine—and layer the entire floor with several thicknesses of newspaper. When the puppy awakens from sleep, and after each feeding, carry him to the papered area. The moment he performs—you won't have long to wait—tell him how pleased you are. Gradually he will associate your approval with the feel of the paper beneath him and will know exactly what you want him to do.

After the puppy has used the paper, roll up all but one sheet of the soiled pile and discard the rest. Layer the area with clean paper, placing the soiled sheet beneath the fresh pile. Dogs are drawn to the smells of elimination and the soiled newspaper will lure the puppy back to that spot. In that way, you condition him to use the paper in one specific area of the room.

Within a week, he probably will be hooked on that spot and run to it automatically. That's your cue to start reducing the floor space you cover, until, in a matter of days, you confine the paper to the chosen location.

Since the very young puppy's bladder and bowel control is weak, he will have to eliminate frequently. When you're not at home, confine him to the papered room. When you're in the house, however, you may allow him to run free, as long as you keep a watchful eye. Place the shake can within arm's reach. The moment your puppy starts to eliminate in another room, shake the can and call out firmly, "No." He will be startled and stop. Carry him immediately into the papered room. When he completes his elimination, praise him lavishly. Note: If the dog has eliminated in areas other than the designated one, apply an odor neutralizer. Two common brands are Super CD and Nilodor, diluted ten drops to three quarts of hot water. Go over all affected areas.

As you get to know your puppy, you will come to learn his preliminary signals. If he begins to walk in circles or sniffs the floor, or if he simply squats, pick him up quickly and carry him to the papered room. Follow his performance with praise.

Paper-training has several undeniable advantages for the owner of a lightweight dog. You need never walk him in inclement weather. You will never feel the wrath of irate pedestrians who object to dog droppings in the street. Paper-training is not recommended, however, for middle- and heavyweight dogs, for obvious reasons. Let's face it, owners of such dogs must resign themselves to housebreaking.

HOUSEBREAKING

Until the dog is twelve weeks old and has completed his innoculation shots, he cannot be taken onto surburban roads or city streets. In the meantime, you must cope with the problem indoors. Confine him to a room with paper, but do not paper-train him. Confusing? I'll explain.

As in paper-training, spread several thicknesses of paper on the floor in one room. Plan to keep the puppy there most of the day. When he eliminates, pick up all the sheets of soiled paper and start over. Do not praise him for using the paper. You do not want to build up the association in his mind that using the paper is what pleases you. If he gets that idea, it will be harder eventually to housebreak him. When you are at home, allow him some brief periods of freedom throughout the house, provided you watch him. If, despite your watchfulness, he has an accident in another area, do not correct him. Grin and bear it. Tick off the days on the calendar. Soon he will reach his twelve-week birthday and you will be able to proceed with his housebreaking.

The schedule for housebreaking the three-month-old puppy is as follows:

Walk him when you awake in the morning.
Walk him after his breakfast, lunch, and dinner.
Walk him before you retire at night.

In order to hasten the housebreaking period, you must adhere to a rigid schedule. Feed him the same kind of food, in the same amounts, at the same times each day. This will encourage his digestive and elimination system to work on a regular basis.

When he has an accident indoors, you must wash away the telltale smell. The odors of elimination lure back the dog and make him more apt to repeat these accidents in the same spot. Cleaning products such as ammonia or detergents are not effective. They may satisfy your aesthetic sense, but to the dog's sensitive nose, the odor remains. Purchase an odor neutralizer, as previously described.

Do not scold your pet after his accident; just mop it up. However, if you are lucky enough to catch him in the act, be ready to correct him. Keep the leash and shake can handy. As the dog starts to squat, shake the can and call out "No." When he stops, attach his leash, rush him outdoors, and allow him to complete his mission along the curb in the street or a designated area of the yard. Follow with effusive praise.

When you take him on his regular housebreaking walks, stay out only long enough for him to relieve himself. Bear in mind that the young puppy may urinate once, walk on for several minutes, then urinate again. Praise him each time he performs. When he has had a double chance to relieve himself, head back to the house. Do not continue down the block for a leisurely half-hour stroll. You are trying, during this period, to have him associate the act of elimination with the curb on the street or an area of the yard. A half hour of continued walking *after* he relieves himself will involve him with a variety of scents and sounds and encounters. He will soon forget the real reason you took him outdoors.

You can give him the exercise he needs with a period of indoor play. Let him chase you back and forth through the house, or toss him a small rubber ball to fetch and carry. But be prepared to take him out immediately afterward, as such play can stimulate his need to urinate. Once he is housebroken and understands the prime reason for your daily trips outdoors, you may proceed to walk and exercise him as well.

There is nothing difficult about learning the housebreaking procedure and how to schedule it on a daily basis. What can be difficult is *being there* to walk the dog.

What do you do when your puppy is very young and unable to control himself for more than a few hours while you, a working person, must be out of the house or apartment all day?

Perhaps you are lucky enough to have an obliging neighbor. If not, an easy answer is a dog-walking service. If you can afford such a service, it will give you great peace of mind. By adhering to your rigid schedule, the dog-walking service will actually shorten the time it takes to housebreak a dog.

If the puppy must remain alone for some eight hours during the day, use a puppy gate and confine him to a small, uncarpeted area. Dogs are fastidious about their elimination habits and do not like to remain in an area that they have just soiled. They would rather make their deposits in one room and then run into another to play. If you keep your dog in close quarters he will make a greater effort to avoid elimination. In the process, he is learning to control and strengthen his bowel and bladder movements.

How well the dog controls himself during the long hours at home alone depends partly on his diet. Do not serve him a seven-course banquet in the morning. The pressure on his bloated belly throughout the day will force him to urinate and defecate long before you arrive home. Keep his breakfast down to a sensible minimum. Apply the same caution to his intake of fluids. While he must have adequate water, do not fill his water dish to the brim. Instead, loosen a tray of ice cubes and toss them into his partially filled water dish just before you walk out the door. The melting cubes will resupply him with water gradually, spacing his intake over a longer period of time.

City-Country Differences

If a puppy has remained alone for an extended period, or awakens from a long sleep with an overwhelming urge to eliminate, one must often act quickly.

Time at such moments is important, and the country owner has the advantage. He snaps on his dog's leash, rushes him out the side door, and within seconds has guided him to the right corner of the yard or down the path to the road.

Not so the city owner. When he leaves his apartment, he has to negotiate the hallway, wait for an elevator, squire his puppy through the lobby, and lead him across the sidewalk and over to the curb.

31

How do you control your impatient puppy? Carry him! Cradled in your arms, he will find it difficult to give in to his urge to relieve himself. Do not set him down until you reach the safety of the paved road. Then, when he performs, give him exuberant praise.

If you're a country owner, you have another recourse. You can train your puppy to eliminate in some area on your property. The one requirement is that it be an enclosed area. A fenced-in yard is ideal.

Walk him into the yard on a regular schedule and keep him outdoors only long enough for him to perform. You may be tempted to allow him to remain outdoors afterward, especially when he is frolicking and amusing himself in a place where you know he is safe. But if you want your training to succeed, follow the standard housebreaking procedure. Wait for him to perform, praise him enthusiastically, and whisk him back indoors. Once he understands that elimination takes place only in the yard, you may leave him outside for longer periods of time.

If it isn't feasible to enclose your yard, you can purchase and set up a run. It should be at least four feet wide and twenty feet long, allowing your dog adequate room to move about.

The puppy who remains on his own property doesn't come in contact with the elimination of other dogs, which reduces the risk of exposure to disease. With the approval of your vet, you may be able to start your dog's housebreaking training at eight or nine weeks, several weeks before he has completed all his shots.

But keep in mind the time of year and your breed of dog. A warm spring day is fine for any puppy; cold weather is not. Your two-month-old hunting or working dog may relish a romp with Jack Frost; your Maltese or Yorkshire is best kept by the fire for another month.

6

CHEWING

PUT TWO DOG owners together and they are apt to swap stories about the eccentric chewing habits of their dogs. "My dog loves shoes," says one owner, "but for some reason, she chews one shoe only and then goes looking for another pair."

"You think that's something," says the other. "My dog chews only the middle two fingers on all my gloves."

A chewing dog may provide you with some intriguing cocktail-party conversation, but unless you are prepared to go through life hopping on one shod foot or are willing to risk frostbite in those ungloved fingers, a dog who chews soon becomes an intolerable nuisance and an unbearable expense.

The chewing tastes of a dog can be as varied as the kinds of cloth and furniture in your home. There are dogs who dote on leather, dogs who are hung up on wool, dogs who are paper freaks, and dogs who are addicted to wood. The dog who refuses to eat canned meat may get his kicks from crunching the can.

Why does a dog chew? Many puppies develop the habit at about seven weeks of age, when they are cutting their permanent set of teeth. Their gums become swollen and tender, and chewing alleviates the pain.

Dog owners are usually sympathetic during this period. They attempt to be helpful by tossing their pup old shoes or socks to nibble on. They are confident that when his permanent teeth emerge, his need to chew will disappear.

Not so. A dog who is allowed to chew old clothes as a puppy may very well develop a permanent appetite for those items and continue the habit into a ripe old age. A dog cannot distinguish between the items you don't mind if he destroys and the items you do. Leather is leather to your dog, and if you toss him an out-of-fashion sandal to munch on, he will assume it's all right to go after your brand-new platform pumps.

What do you do, then, when your puppy is teething, when he whimpers piteously and his eyes meet yours with that suffering look?

Put some ice cubes in his water dish. The cold will numb his gums and ease his pain. Another solution is to soak a washcloth in cold water, freeze it, then give it to the dog so he can chew on it for the same soothing effect. Or purchase a rawhide toy and rub it with bacon fat. Rawhide is edible and the bacon aroma will keep him chewing contentedly for a long period of time. Stay away from toys made of soft rubber. Your puppy can bite off a chunk and the rubber may lodge in his throat or intestines. Chewing on a bone is another method of relief. If you are serving a robust vegetable soup to the family, remove the marrow bones and set them aside for your dog. But don't offer him the steak and chicken bones left over from your dinner plate. These can splinter or break, and a jagged end may cause serious if not fatal damage to a dog.

If, after his permanent teeth come through, your dog continues to chew, what then? You must catch him red-handed and correct him immediately.

Entrapment can be fair play in this case. If his favorite chewing object is something small—a paperback book, perhaps—drop it to the floor. Stay in the room and keep your shake can handy (but do not let the dog see it). You may read the newspaper or talk on the phone, but remain alert to your dog's actions. Sooner or later he will sense that your attention is elsewhere, sidle up to the planted object, and pounce on it.

At that moment, shake the can vigorously and call out "No." Your dog will no doubt be startled and back away. Rush to his side, pat him, and tell him what a grand fellow he is.

When he is alone in the house, or if he prefers objects larger than can be left on the floor, you can correct him by making the items unpalatable. If he is fond of the legs of your kitchen table, coat them with a bitter-tasting substance. There are several commercial products, such as Alum (in its powder form) or Bitter Apple, that are available in pet and drugstores for this purpose. Or you may prefer to whip up a homemade concoction. Choose among such ingredients as mustard, tabasco sauce, cayenne pepper, and curry powder, and mix them into a paste. Before you leave the house, put your dog in the same room with the baited item. One bite should convince your puppy that they just don't make table legs the way they used to. (If you suspect that your dog has a sensitive stomach, check with your veterinarian before trying this method.)

Dogs sometimes resort to chewing out of frustration. The dog that is left alone all day frequently becomes restless, lonely, and bored. What better way to pass the long, sedentary hours than by chewing up the house?

The first thing to do is consider his daily exercise schedule. Perhaps he needs a more extensive physical workout before you leave each morning.

If you suspect that he is lonely, switch on the radio before you leave the house. Keep the volume low. The soft music and the subdued tones of the announcer may have a soothing effect on your dog.

Or perhaps the problem rests with his diet. Ocassionally a dog chews simply because he is hungry. If you are housebreaking your dog, you do not want to overload him with food in the morning, but you must not go to the other extreme and give him a substandard breakfast. If you think he may be hungry, serve him a larger portion of food each morning. With a substantial breakfast sticking to his ribs, his craving for a midmorning chunk of lampshade may well disappear.

CITY-COUNTRY DIFFERENCES

Out in the country, you may run into a different kind of chewing problem. If your puppy comes of teething age during mild or warm weather and you have a fenced-in yard, you may very well avoid all the chewing problems of the city owner. A dog who remains out in the yard all day doesn't have much chance to savor the delights of your damask drapes.

He may, however, develop a taste for your plants and shrubs.

The best way to nip this habit in the bud, so to speak, is to come upon him red-handed and correct him immediately.

One method of correction is the shake can. Swing the kitchen door open for your dog. While he scampers out, reach for your can, walk to the kitchen window, and watch and wait. Be certain that your dog cannot see you. When he gets within sniffing distance of the azalea bush that he has been working over for a day or two, sprint to the door and throw the can. Aim the can *near* him but not *at* him. Accompany the sound of the clanking can with a stern "No." As he freezes to a stop, walk outside and praise him. Then pick up the shake can and go back to your post at the kitchen window. He may have learned that the azaleas are not on his menu, but what about those chrysanthemums a few yards away? Be ready once again to toss the can and use your drill-sergeant voice. When he complies, praise him warmly.

If stronger methods are required, use the corrective jerk. Attach a clothesline to your dog's collar and walk outdoors with him. Pay out the line and peek around from behind a corner of the house. Leave enough slack in the line so that your dog is free to move about. As he approaches the mums, give a firm jerk on the line and call out "No." Then run to his side and praise him. Note: This procedure works equally well for another country problem—digging in the yard. Try the shake can method first. If, despite your efforts with the can, your dog seems bent on digging his way to China, get out the clothesline and use the long-range corrective jerk.

7

BARKING

EVERYONE WANTS a dog that barks on occasion; nobody wants a dog that barks too much. Your dog, doing what comes naturally, will bark when the doorbell rings and when a stranger enters the house. That's fine, he is performing his duty of protecting your hearth and home. But if he continues to howl long after you have answered the door and told him to be quiet, he is making a nuisance of himself.

The shake can is frequently helpful in correcting this situation. As you walk to the door, tell him he's a good boy for alerting you and then call "Quiet!" (The reason you don't use "No!" is to avoid any association in the dog's mind of barking itself being bad. You just want him to stop after the first time or two.) If he resumes his ululations when you open the door, jiggle the can and tell him "Quiet!" once again. Or toss the can onto the floor beside him.

If sterner measures are required, enlist the aid of another person and use the corrective jerk. Attach your dog's leash and collar and have a friend or neighbor ring your bell. When the dog barks, praise him for sounding the initial alarm and then tell him "Quiet!" If he insists upon having the last word, jerk the leash quickly and firmly and repeat your "Quiet!" Be sure to praise him when he stops.

Another problem is the dog that barks when left alone in the house. He may bark for any of several reasons: He may be lonely and frightened; he may feel restless and confined; the phone may ring and set him off; he may hear noises in the hall or outside; he may even be hungry.

An early-morning play session will work off some of his excess energy, and a puppy gate in the doorway of his room will make him feel less confined. If you plan to return home after sunset, be sure to switch a light on in his room before you leave. You can keep the radio playing softly, and you can provide him with a supply of rawhide toys. And if you suspect that he barks because he is hungry, you can increase the food you give him for breakfast.

Frequently, after a full weekend with his owner, a dog can experience withdrawal symptoms when his owner leaves for work Monday morning. If you get more complaints from your neighbors early in the week, you can be sure your dog is suffering from a separation syndrome.

As difficult as it may be, do not give him your undivided attention over the weekend. Instead, for brief periods of time, leave him alone in a room. It will help condition and prepare him for the Blue Monday ahead.

It can also give you a chance to catch him in the act of barking and correct him. The first time he barks while he's alone in the kitchen of your apartment (behind a baby or puppy gate, not a closed door) and you're watching TV in the living room, jiggle the shake can and call out a firm "No!" It may be necessary to go one step further and toss the can in front of the kitchen doorway. If he continues to bark, you must resort to the corrective jerk. Attach his collar and tie a long clothesline to it. Pay out the line leaving enough slack so that you don't put tension on the dog, and go back to the living room. But don't get too immersed in your TV program. Be prepared at the first sounds from the kitchen to jerk the line and call out "No!" The moment his barking stops, congratulate him with a loud and exuberant "Good boy!"

Once he learns to stay alone without barking while you are in another part of the house, you can teach him not to bark after you leave.

Get up fifteen minutes earlier than usual and go through your Monday-morning ritual. When you pick up your handbag or reach for your attaché case, your dog will no doubt recognize that the moment of parting has arrived. Pat him good-bye and walk out the front door. Take the shake can with you and leave the front door unlocked. Walk about twenty feet from the door, then stand and wait. If your dog has taken to barking when left alone, chances are he'll start vocalizing within a few minutes. Dash back into the house or apartment, rattle the shake can, and call out a firm "No!" For added effect, toss the shake can to the floor. Walk out once again, and be prepared to repeat the procedure.

If several attempts do not produce results, move on to the corrective technique. Put on your dog's collar and attach a long clothesline. Grab the other end of the line and take up your post outside the door. The moment he starts his solo, jerk the line firmly and call out a loud and clear "No." Congratulate him when he stops. Note: If the clothesline is too thick to allow you to close the door, use a fishline instead. Be certain to wear a pair of sturdy gloves.

Barking can also be a problem when you take your dog outdoors. The presence of a stranger on a suburban road, the sound of a car screeching down a city street, the sudden appearance of another dog—any of these may prove upsetting to your pet and trigger his desire to bark. Since your dog is on his leash, you are already prepared to execute a correction. Hold on to the leash as you walk down the street and keep him close to your side. At the first yelp from your dog, jerk the leash quickly and firmly and tell him "No." Follow the correction with enthusiastic praise.

City-Country Differences

City living exposes your dog to a special variety of noises—neighbors chatting in the hallway as they wait for the elevator, a record player blaring in the next apartment, or children running across the floor in the apartment overhead.

In order to decrease these distractions while you are gone, keep your dog in a room that is set back from the hallway and farthest from any noisy neighbor. If your building has a doorman, alert him when you leave so that your doorbell is not rung while you are out. Tell him to hold any packages that arrive for you in the lobby instead of dropping them in front of your door. By keeping your dog in a quiet room and minimizing the chances of any sudden noise, you cut down the chances of his becoming excited and barking.

In the country, there are dogs that bark incessantly in their own backyard. Few neighbors object to sporadic barking. They understand that your pet is apt to bark when the mailman approaches, when the newsboy aims the afternoon paper at your front step, or when a youngster pedals past the house on a ten-speed Schwinn. But neighbors will complain when a dog starts barking an hour before their alarm is set to go off, or displays its baritone prowess for hours at a stretch.

Why does a dog howl incessantly when outdoors? Chances are he is physically confined or noisy distractions are around, e.g., other dogs or children, etc. If you don't have a fenced-in yard, do not make the mistake of tying him to a stake on a short leash. It is frustrating for him to dash forward a few steps and then be jolted to a stop. Instead, use a tie-out stake, available from your local pet shop. This will usually satisfy his need to move about freely.

8

Jumping on People

MANY OWNERS have a double standard about dogs jumping on people. They think jumping is cute in a puppy but, like thumbsucking in a child, to be outgrown when the puppy matures. And there are others who think it's all right for their mature pet to jump under *certain* circumstances, on *particular* people, at *specific* times.

The trouble with this sometimes-yes-sometimes-no philosophy is that it doesn't work. If your dog is allowed to jump on you when he is a puppy, he will continue to do so when he is fully grown. If he is allowed to hurl himself at you when you enter the house, he will hurl himself at your frail old grandmother when she comes to call. And if he is allowed to leap into your lap while you talk on the phone, he will also leap into your lap while you are drinking hot coffee.

Why does the young puppy jump up to greet you? He wants to reach you. He sees your face several feet above him and hears your voice coming from somewhere up in the clouds; he is eager to get closer to both you and your voice.

When you arrive home, set your evening paper aside and drop to a crouch beside your pet. Eyeball to eyeball, talk softly and soothingly to him. He will gradually learn that he can greet you affectionately and command your full attention while keeping all four paws on the ground.

If he has attained his full growth and still lunges at you every time you come home, do not despair. It is not too late to correct him.

Get out your shake can and walk out the door. Wait at least five minutes before you reenter the house. The moment your dog jumps, jounce the can firmly and call out "No!" Then tell him he's a good boy. Follow your praise by reaching forward and patting him. Give him several minutes to tail-wag his welcome. You do not want to discourage the dog from greeting you, but rather to change the manner in which he does it.

You will have to repeat this procedure several days in a row. If your dog proves stubborn or slow to learn, you will have to find an aide and move on to the corrective jerk.

Arrange for a family member or close friend to be waiting on your return home, with the dog's leash and collar attached. When you enter the house and your dog catapults into the air, have your accomplice jerk the leash and call out "No!" Be ready to give your pet a long and loving greeting.

A dog hooked on jumping will fly at anyone who enters the house. Some owners lock their dog in the bedroom when they are expecting guests. This creates several problems. The dog is apt to howl all evening, drowning out much of your dinner-party chatter. And woe to the unsuspecting guest who opens the wrong door while searching for the bathroom.

It is imperative that you teach your dog not to jump on others. Pick up the shake can when the doorbell rings. As your first visitor enters and the dog rises into the air, jiggle the can vigorously and call out "No!" Praise him lavishly. Repeat this procedure as each new guest arrives.

If several attempts do not bring results, attach your dog's leash and collar. When he hurls himself at the next person to arrive, jerk the leash firmly and shout out "No!" Follow this with enthusiastic praise.

If you'd just as soon not hold a dog-training session the night of a party, set up a practice situation in advance. Ask a friend to ring your doorbell. When the dog jumps, administer the corrective jerk. Be sure to follow this with praise. It may be necessary for your friend to walk out of the house, ring the doorbell, and reenter several times.

CITY-COUNTRY DIFFERENCES

If you're a city owner, your dog comes in close contact with many strangers. When you leave your apartment, for example, the elevator you enter may be filled with people. Such proximity to others may prove an irresistible temptation to your pet.

Since your dog is wearing his leash and collar for his outdoor walk, you are in a position to correct him. Shorten the leash to prepare yourself for the corrective jerk. The moment he makes a move upward, jerk the leash firmly and say "No." Tell him immediately what a good dog he is.

Some passengers in the elevator may actively encourage the dog to jump. "Here, pal," they say, patting their thigh to entice the dog. You will have to tell them, firmly and simply, that your dog is not allowed to jump. Not on anyone, not at any time.

The same technique applies when you are out on

the street. If you stop at the corner to wait for a light, shorten your grip on his leash. If he lunges at the stranger standing alongside you, give him a correction, tell him "No," and follow this with immediate praise.

A word of caution: In my discussion of exercise I stressed the importance of running and jumping. If your dog has a jumping-on-people problem, do not toss balls into the air for him to retrieve. If you encourage him to leap for the ball and, at the same time, scold him for leaping onto you, he may well become confused. Correct the jumping problem first. Once he is trained not to jump on people, you may introduce ball-catching to him. He will then associate his jumping with your throwing something and will confine his leaping to the daily play period with you.

9

JUMPING ON FURNITURE

OWNERS ARE frequently guilty of encouraging their dogs to jump on furniture. If you pick up your puppy and hold him in your lap as you sit on a sofa, your puppy will assume he has squatter's rights and will soon hop onto the sofa by himself. As much as you would like to cuddle him, you must never sit down and cradle the puppy in your lap. Instead, allow your pet to snuggle close to your feet while you reach down and gently pat him, or get down to his own level and dispense your affection there.

If your dog is full-grown and accustomed to jumping on furniture, it is not too late to break him of the habit. Try the shake can method first. If, after several attempts, he continues to ignore the jouncing of the can and remains impervious to your stern "No," use the corrective jerk. Attach his collar and tie a long clothesline to it. Pay out the line and allow the dog to wander freely about the room. The moment he heads up into his favorite chair, jerk the clothesline firmly and tell him "No." Congratulate him when he complies.

A wily dog, aware of your disapproval, will wait until you leave the house and then sneak onto your bed. When you arrive home, he is back on the floor with an innocent look in his eyes. But the telltale signs are there: a crumpled pillow, scratches on the wooden headboard, a cluster of dog hairs on the spread.

You have to catch him red-handed and startle him . . . even though you are not at home! One solution is to set up a half dozen mousetraps underneath a layer or two of taped newspaper. When your dog jumps onto the bed, the traps will go off. They cannot hurt the dog, but the sudden clatter will come as a distinctly unpleasant shock.

If he prefers to sleep on the couch, set the traps there, cover the area the dog uses with newspaper, and tape the ends of the paper to the couch.

You find mousetraps unappealing? Use shake cans instead. Tie several to a wire long enough to string across the bed or table or chair. Tape both ends of the wire to the furniture. The clinking sound of the cans at the moment your dog jumps up and strikes them will no doubt bewilder him. He'll probably bolt to the other end of the room.

Or instead of the cans, use party balloons. Tie them in clusters along the wire. The dog's sharp claws will burst the balloons when he jumps onto the furniture, and he will turn tail and run. If you want to make this preeffective, burst a balloon in his presence, and while he's watching you, still impressed by the effect, tie some others along the wire. Chances are he will stay clear. But with balloons, some words of caution: Don't use them with a shy or nervous dog. And don't try them if the dog has shown any appetite for rubber, which can prove harmful if ingested.

Repeat these procedures as many times as necessary. One evening you will arrive home to find the mousetraps unsprung or the throw cans and balloons undisturbed. If you are a practical sort, you may keep the mousetraps for their original purpose. If you feel like celebrating your success, take a pin and burst the balloons yourself.

10

Going into Garbage

THE BEST WAY to prevent this problem is to keep your garbage pail covered and concealed in a kitchen cabinet or closet. Some dogs, however, are cunning enough to pry open the door and nose the lid off the pail. Once the pail is exposed, its contents are as tempting to your pet as the apple was to Eve. He is apt to throw caution to the wind, forget his table manners, and dig right in.

The results can be disastrous. Apple cores and coffee grounds soon litter the kitchen floor. Or he may haul his loot around the house and those last drops in the tomato juice can will sink into your living-room rug. But what sinks into the dog's stomach may be most damaging of all. The combination of banana peels and cellophane wrappers may make him reel in discomfort and regurgitate the entire feast. Or, much worse, those empty tuna fish cans may cut his mouth and the chicken bones may pierce his throat. Going into garbage is a habit that can prove fatal and must be stopped.

If you are at home, catch him in the act and correct him. Put some raw meat or other tempting morsel into the pail and walk out of the kitchen. Have your shake can handy and wait in another room. As soon as your dog plunges into the pail, dash into the room, shake the can vigorously, and shout "No!" As he comes to a reluctant halt, tell him how much you admire his self-control.

If your dog is a confirmed garbage hound, use the corrective jerk. Attach the dog's collar and tie a clothesline to it. Pay out the line and allow your dog to move about freely. You may busy yourself with nearby chores, but keep one eye on your dog. When he heads toward the pail with quivering nostrils, pull sharply on the clothesline and tell him "No!" Be sure to follow this correction with praise.

If you are not going to be at home, don't leave a bagful of garbage in your pail. Drop the bag down the incinerator or, if you are out in the country, deposit it in your outdoor pail. But, while this removes the temptation, it doesn't really teach the dog that pawing at the garbage is wrong. To convince him firmly and forever that the pail is off limits, you have to persuade him that the contents of the pail are vile tasting and certainly not fit for a dog to eat.

The same preparation that you used to correct your dog's chewing problem is appropriate here. Purchase some Alum (in its powder form) or Bitter Apple. Or fix a homemade witches' brew by combining tabasco sauce, cayenne pepper, mustard, and any other spicy condiment you have in your pantry.

Apply the preparation around the lid of the garbage pail. As he tries to get past it, your dog will screw up his face like a child tasting cod-liver oil for the first time.

CITY-COUNTRY PROBLEMS

In the suburbs, your dog may be lured by your outside pail or by pails in your neighbors' yards. Correction calls for the same methods you use indoors.

Try the shake can first. Rush into the yard, rattle the can, and call out "No!" Or toss the can near his feet.

If necessary, use the corrective jerk. Attach a clothesline to the dog's collar and conceal yourself around a corner of the house. Remember to wear a pair of sturdy gloves. Be ready to execute a long-range correction and follow it with praise.

In the city, your dog may head for a trash basket as you walk down the street. Correct him with the leash and a "No." Praise him warmly.

11

CAR CHASING

IF YOUR DOG could write his own Declaration of Independence, it would proclaim his inalienable right to life, liberty, and the pursuit of cars. The dog who lives in an apartment and is walked on a leash doesn't get much opportunity to chase cars, but the country dog certainly does. Indoors or out in the yard he is close to street noises, and the squeal of a tire or the roar of an engine can set his chasing juices going. If you happen to answer the doorbell or open the yard gate as a car careens down the block, your dog may well rush past you and out the door in full pursuit of the moving vehicle.

This habit frequently proves fatal to the dog. Sometimes, as the driver swerves to avoid the dog, it causes human injury and property damage as well. It is a habit that, once allowed to develop, is difficult to break, but nevertheless one that must be stopped.

It is necessary to catch him in the act and correct him. Attach his leash and collar and tie a clothesline to the leash. Plan to have a friend drive past your house. As the car rolls down your block, pick up the other end of the clothesline and open the door. Let your dog take off for some twenty-five or thirty feet, then execute a very strong correction accompanied by a sharp "No!" The long-distance jerk may knock him over on his back, like a flipped pancake, but it is absolutely necessary to be firm, even harsh. As he scrambles back to his feet and turns a puzzled look in your direction, shower him with praise.

A dog doesn't give up car chasing easily, and it may be necessary to repeat this procedure many times.

Another way to break him of the habit is to have the correction come from within the moving car. Arrange for a passenger in the back seat to toss a shake can at your dog's feet as he races up to the car, with a loud simultaneous "No!" Congratulate your dog when he stops. Or equip the passenger with a pitcher of water to throw over your dog, or a water pistol to squirt at him. While he is shaking himself dry, tell him what a fine and obedient fellow he is.

12

Miscellaneous Problems

More Than One Dog

IF YOUR DOG gets frightened or bored when left alone, with chronic misbehavior as a result, giving him a playmate is often a solution. You can, however, run into initial difficulties in such cases, especially if the new dog is a puppy. Give the older dog an extra dollop of attention to reassure him that the newcomer hasn't replaced him in your affections. In time, he will welcome the new dog as a companion.

Two cautions: Do not put an older dog and a new puppy together in the same room until the puppy is housebroken; if the older dog comes within sniffing distance of the puppy's elimination, he is apt to forget his own training and add to the mess on the floor. And whenever you have a command or a correction, make sure you clearly communicate which dog is intended.

A Change in Environment

Dogs that move with their families from the city to the country usually thrive on the change. The suburbs may not have the cosmopolitan atmosphere that your dog-of-the-world is accustomed to, but the freedom to run loose in a yard and chase robins and blue jays soon compensates for the loss of the daily walks down bustling city streets.

When you reverse the procedure, however, moving from the country to the city, your dog is apt to have some negative reactions. It is tough to give up roaming through a large home or over spacious grounds and adjust to confinement in close living quarters. Some dogs go berserk, forget all their training and manners, and wreak havoc in the new apartment.

A dog in such a situation should be given an abundance of exercise. Take long walks with him several times daily. Get over to a playground and throw balls for him to retrieve. If he works off his excess energy in these extended play periods, he will find it easier to relax and settle for his new sedentary life the rest of the day.

Initially he may be lonely and frightened at being left alone in an apartment. During the first few weeks, spend as much time as possible with him at home. Your presence will reassure him that he hasn't been abandoned to some strange, confined environment.

If he is used to the quiet lanes of suburbia he may also have difficulty adjusting to the fracas of city streets. Autos honking, fire sirens wailing, trucks rumbling down the street, and clusters of people chatting at street corners—this new hubbub may startle and frighten him. Introduce him to it gradually. Take him out very early in the morning or late in the evening when distractions are at a minimum. Slowly, as he becomes accustomed to the action on city streets, gradually work your walking schedule into the noisier hours of the day.

Familiarize him with his new environment in gradual stages, provide him with ample exercise, and give him lots of attention—these are the measures that will ease the difficult period of transition from country to city.

III

Basic Obedience Training

13

Introduction

Up to now you have been teaching your dog *not* to do certain things: chew up the drapes, jump on furniture, etc. It is just as important to teach him the things he *must* do: obey your commands.

He must drop into the "Sit" position when you tell him to. He must go "Down" at your command. He must "Heel" when accompanying you outdoors. And he must respond immediately when you call him to "Come."

This section presents a step-by-step program for teaching these commands to your dog. The program is twofold: The early stages concentrate on formal training sessions; the later stages move on to practical application. The practical application reinforces his understanding of the commands and teaches him that he must obey them under all circumstances, regardless of distractions—in any place, at any time.

How long it takes to teach the entire course depends on your dog's age and temperament. A dog that is very young or very active or very strong willed may need several months to learn what is expected of him; a dog ten months or older with a responsive, eager-to-please nature may zip through the course in a mere five weeks.

It is important that you conduct daily practice sessions. If you are working with a three-month-old puppy, keep your training periods limited to five minutes; a dog six months or older may be worked for fifteen minutes at a stretch.

During the early stages of training, eliminate as many distractions as possible. Do not feed your dog before a training session—he may become too drowsy to concentrate. And be certain he has recently had a walk to relieve himself. Choose a quiet corner of the house, your yard, or some other semi-enclosed area in which to work. Do not allow any member of the family to watch on the sidelines or offer advice. Remember, you want your dog's undivided attention.

The commands you will be teaching him include "Sit," "Stay," "Heel," "Down," and "Come." And no vocabulary of command words is complete without the word "Okay." "Okay" is used to release your dog from a command. When you want to release him from his "Sit" position, you tell him "Okay." When you want to give him permission to step out of the "Heel" position and seek the curb, you tell him "Okay." And you use it to let him know that the training session is over.

You may discover that your dog learns some commands faster than others, or that he finds one phase of a command easier to comprehend than the next. No matter. Just don't rush his training. Stay with each step of a command until he understands it fully. When he performs it properly for the first time, repeat it at least half a dozen times before moving on to the next step. And in subsequent sessions, run him through everything he has learned before taking up a new step.

It is this constant repetition that strengthens his understanding and leads to successful and enduring results.

14

"Sit - Stay"

YOUR FRONT DOOR is a gateway to endless fascination for your dog. Several times daily he accompanies you through it and out into the street for his elimination and exercise walks. Beyond it, he encounters many strange people, a variety of foreign noises, and an overwhelming assortment of exotic scents. The door is his "Open sesame" into a world filled with adventure and surprise.

Is it any wonder that, when you open the door to answer the bell, your pet whizzes past you and your caller and makes a beeline for the great outdoors?

What do you do? Do you shout, "No, bad dog, come back!" Do you take off in hot pursuit? No, you simply do not allow the problem to occur. You command him to "Sit" before you open the door.

Sitting comes easily to your dog. He squats on his haunches for brief periods of rest throughout his busy day. He sits when he wants to, and wherever he chooses.

So now you are going to teach him to "Sit" at your

command—wherever he happens to be. And you will teach him to remain in the "Sit" position—to "Stay"—until you release him from the command.

Step One: "Sit"

Attach the collar and leash to your dog and slip your right thumb through the loop at the end of the leash.

Stand to the right of the dog so that both of you are facing in the same direction.

In teaching this command you must keep the leash short. Reach down with your left hand, grasp the leash approximately four feet from the loop, carry it over to the right, and wrap it around your right thumb on top of the loop. The leash should now stretch across the front of your body in a straight line between the dog's collar and your right hand, with only enough slack to avoid any pull on the dog. You are ready to begin.

Teaching "Sit" requires that you do two things simultaneously.

First, call out "Sit." Draw the word out—"Si-i-i-t" —and say it in a low and soothing tone. Your dog responds to the *tone* of your voice, and if you say "Sit" quickly it tends to come out sharp and harsh. Use just the word "Sit." You would only confuse him with "I want you to be a good boy now, Marvin, and sit." Or even, "Marvin, sit." In this training program the dog's name is used exclusively as a signal for him to move forward.

At the same moment that you call out "Sit," turn toward the dog and use both hands to guide him into the "Sit" position. With your left hand, press down gently but firmly on the dog's rump; with your right hand, pull up on the leash to keep it taut so that the

Figures 4, 5, 6. "Sit": Leash taut, left hand on rump; pull up with right hand, push down with left; command completed.

dog cannot move out of position or drop his head (but not so tight that you frighten or hurt him).

The pressure of your left hand forces the dog to squat on his haunches; the leash action of your right hand keeps the front of his body upright and his forelegs straight. Your two hands work simultaneously in a seesaw motion: Left hand presses *down*, right hand pulls *up*.

Once he is "Sitting," praise him warmly. It doesn't matter that you have maneuvered him into position. Let him know what a "Good dog!" he is for obeying your command.

After a while you will find it unnecessary to exert any physical pressure on your dog; he will drop into the "Sit" position at the sound of your command. How long it takes him to do this depends on several factors—age, temperament, and breed. Some dogs understand the command "Sit" by the end of the first practice session; others need daily practice sessions for several days in a row.

When you have him dropping into the "Sit" position without any physical pressure from you, eliminate the use of your hands. Stand to the right of the dog and call out "Sit." Do not touch the dog and do not pull on the leash. Give him a few seconds to comply before repeating the command, and several repetitions without reaction before you resort to hard pressure. And whenever he complies, belt out an enthusiastic "Good boy!"

If he gets through a session in which he responds properly without hand pressure a dozen times in a row, he is ready to move on to step two.

STEP TWO: "SIT-STAY"

Review step one. Put the dog in the "Sit" position and praise him when he complies.

Now, call out the command "Stay." As with "Sit," draw out the word—"Sta-a-a-y." Keep your tone encouraging and soft.

At the same moment you call out "Stay," pass your left hand momentarily in front of the dog's eyes. Do not touch his face; simply block his vision for an instant. Blocking his vision helps connect the idea of remaining in place with the word "Stay."

Next, turn and face your dog in the following way: Step forward and to the left with your *right* foot and, keeping your left foot in place, swivel on the balls of both feet to execute a quick about-face; once you make this full turn, bring your left foot against the right one. Note: In this training course, stepping forward on your left foot is a signal for your dog to move forward, so until you are facing the dog and thus blocking his forward movement, do not lift your left foot from the floor.

At the same moment that you execute your about-face, raise the leash high above your dog's head. Hold it slightly to either side so that you do not hit him on the chin with the metal clip. Your dog may wriggle about or strain to move forward, so be certain to keep the leash taut.

Once you are facing the dog, praise him warmly. It does not matter that you are blocking his forward movement or that the leash is holding him in place. Let him know what a bright fellow he is for remaining in "Stay."

Stand before him for about thirty seconds to let him absorb the meaning of the command. Then go back to your original position and start all over.

First, tell him to "Sit" and praise him when he complies. Second, tell him to "Stay" as you swing your left hand briefly in front of his eyes. Third, step in front of him with your right foot and execute an about-face. Be certain to hold the leash taut. Fourth,

Figures 7, 8, 9. "Stay": Give
simultaneous voice and
hand commands; swing
right foot in front of dog,
keeping left foot fixed; pivot
to face dog and bring up left
foot.

stand before him for thirty seconds and praise him warmly. Repeat this drill until he performs it successfully at least a dozen times in a row.

It may take many attempts until your dog understands that he must remain in place. Do not be discouraged. Maintain a calm, patient attitude. Remember, repetition is the key to successful training.

STEP THREE: "SIT-STAY" FROM A DISTANCE OF SIX FEET

Review step two. Put your dog in the "Sit" position and follow this command with "Stay." Execute an about-face to stand before him. Praise him.

Now shift the loop of the leash to your left hand. Place your right hand on the leash approximately two feet from the dog's collar and pull it high and taut above the dog's head. (The remaining four feet of leash dangles loosely between your hands.)

Letting the leash slip through your right hand, take one step backward and stop. Tell your dog to "Stay." Praise him when he does.

Continue to move backward one step at a time. If your pet has lived by the motto "I follow my master wherever he goes," chances are he will leap forward now. You must stop him. The instant he moves, command him to "Stay." At the same moment, take a step forward to block him and shorten the leash through your right hand until it is again high and taut above his head. Once he settles, give him a "Good boy!"

Resume backing away until you reach the end of the six-foot leash. With each step backward, stop and remind your dog to "Stay." Praise him. Note: Keep your praise gentle and calm. If you allow exuberance to creep into your voice, it will excite your dog and he will find it almost impossible to remain in place.

Stand before him for about thirty seconds and allow him to absorb the meaning of "Stay" at the full six-foot distance. Then go back to your original position and start all over. Repeat this until he performs it successfully at least a dozen times in a row.

STEP FOUR: "SIT-STAY" WHILE YOU CIRCLE THE DOG

Review the previous steps. Have him "Sit" and then "Stay." Execute an about-face in front of him and back away the full length of the six-foot leash. Remind him to "Stay." "Atta boy!"

Now, keeping the leash high and taut, move a foot to the right. Stop and praise him. Reverse your direction and move two feet to the left. Congratulate him in a soft and reassuring voice.

Continue to move from side to side, gradually extending the arc of your movement in each direction. You can let your dog turn his head and follow your movements, but if he attempts to turn his body, you must stop him. Step forward, tighten up on the leash, and tell him "Stay."

Walk from side to side a dozen times. Let him know how pleased you are.

Now, slowly start a continuous walk around him. Call out "Stay" in a soft, soothing voice at various points. When you complete a full circle, stop and praise him.

It is important that you hold the leash high and taut while you orbit the dog. If at any point he attempts to move, tighten the leash momentarily and remind him to "Stay." It is this firm control of the leash that communicates to your dog the idea of "Stay."

Complete a full circle a half dozen times in a row. Then give him a short recess. (Maintaining a stationary posture while you repeatedly move around him, disappearing and then reappearing, is hard concentration for your dog.) Allow him to get up and stretch his paws. After a minute, put him back in the "Sit" position and start all over. Circle around him another six times.

It will take a while for your dog to absorb this lesson and understand that he must not move. Each time he comes out of the "Sit" position, you will have to start him from the beginning. Do not be impatient with him. The day will come when he holds his stationary posture throughout an entire training session. You can then move on to the next step.

Step Five: Practical Application with the Leash On

Your dog understands the meaning of "Sit-Stay" within the controlled atmosphere of the training session. Now you want him to respond to your command under everyday circumstances, at any time and in any place.

Attach your dog's collar and leash and walk him toward your front door. Put him in "Sit-Stay." Have a friend or family member ring the bell and open the door.

It is one thing for your dog to follow instructions while the two of you are alone in a room without distractions. But it's almost too much to expect him to resist the sight of an open door. Chances are your dog will leap forward.

Now is the time to use the corrective jerk. Your dog understands the command; he must be "corrected" if he disobeys.

The moment he springs up, call out a sharp "No!" and execute a firm correction with the leash. It does not matter that he is attempting to run forward—jerk the leash to the *right*, exactly as you learned in the chapter on the corrective technique. Tell him once again to "Sit" and "Stay." Shower him with praise when he complies.

Repeat this routine for several days in a row, or until it is no longer necessary to correct your dog.

STEP SIX: "SIT-STAY"
WITHOUT THE LEASH, INDOORS

Go back to your practice room. Attach the dog's collar and leash and run through the entire series of commands. Praise him.

Now drop your end of the leash to the floor. Stand still and tell him "Stay" once again. "Good boy!"

Although you are no longer holding the leash, your dog can see it stretched out on the floor before him. It acts as a psychological deterrent.

Keeping your hands at your sides, move several feet to the left. Reverse your steps and move several feet to the right. Start a slow walk around him. Along the way, remind him repeatedly to "Stay" and continue to tell him what a smart dog he is. Circle and praise him a half dozen times, then give him a well-earned recess. Repeat the entire process.

In your next session, put him in "Sit-Stay," drop his leash to the floor, and walk out of the room. Return in several seconds and praise him if he has not moved. Leave him again, and stay out of the room a bit longer. Work at this until you are able to leave him alone in the "Sit-Stay" position for a full five minutes.

Step Seven: Practical Application Without the Leash, Indoors

The leash is your training tool. Your ultimate goal is to have the dog obey your command when he is not wearing a leash. Once he responds to "Sit-Stay" without any leash control in his practice sessions, use the command from time to time during the day while he is running loose through the house. Tell him to "Sit-Stay" while you are diapering the baby; tell him to "Sit-Stay" while you enjoy a cigar; and, of course, tell him to "Sit-Stay" before you open the door. Always be sure to praise him when he responds correctly.

15

The "Heel"

WHEN YOUR PUPPY was three months old, you probably enjoyed your daily outings as much as he. It gave you pleasure to watch him scamper about on his leash as you walked him down the block. You were amused when he ran forward to greet some youngsters up ahead, or when he suddenly veered to the side to follow some exotic scent.

You had no concern for his safety because you had him on a six-foot leash. He was small, didn't weigh very much, and you felt completely in control.

But now he is six months old and the situation is changing. He is getting heavier and stronger. When he leaps forward, he pulls you with him. When he dashes off to one side, he all but yanks your arm out of its socket. And when he stops to examine some debris on the ground, you cannot budge him, no matter how hard you pull on the leash.

Now it's not so much fun anymore. And what happens if you lose your balance and are thrown to the ground? Or the leash slips from your hand and your dog runs into the road? If he gets any bigger, will you have to give him up?

You must, of course, teach him to "Heel." "Heeling" means walking with the dog by your side, his head close to your thigh. It means matching his steps to yours, whether you stride briskly down the block or amble along at a leisurely pace. It means his following you as you turn to the left or to the right. It means his stopping when you stop, then sitting automatically at your side. And it means that he rises to his feet and trots by your side when you resume your walk.

Heeling goes against your dog's natural instincts and is perhaps the hardest on-leash lesson for him to learn. Do not try to teach him the "Heel" command until he is at least four to five months old. It is unfair to expect a frisky three-month-old puppy to walk sedately by your side. You may succeed in teaching him to do this, of course, but you do so at the risk of your dog's personality. It is wiser to give your dog a few months to mature.

Talk to him in cheerful tones throughout your training sessions. And be exuberant in your praise. You want to convince him that walking by your side is fun.

STEP ONE: WALK IN "HEEL"

Select a training area that allows you sufficient room to walk back and forth. You may work indoors or out, but be certain that the area is quiet and free of distractions. You want your dog's undivided attention.

In the suburbs, an enclosed backyard is fine. So is the basement of your house. In the city, you may choose a long hallway in your apartment house, a schoolyard, or an enclosed area in the park.

Attach his collar and leash and stand to the right of the dog. Tell him to "Sit." Gather up half the leash in your right hand, leaving roughly three feet hanging between your hand and the dog's collar. Let both your arms hang loose at your sides.

Let's say your dog's name is Oliver, You call the command "Oliver, heel." "Heel" is an action command; you want your dog to move forward. Therefore you call out his name just before you issue the command. The sound of the name focuses his attention on you and alerts him to get ready to move.

Put emphasis on the word "Heel." Thus, the command becomes, "Oliver, *heel.*"

As you say "Heel," step forward on your left foot. It is important to start with the left foot. This is the foot next to your dog. Seeing you move forward, he will move forward, too.

Start walking at a slow, measured pace. Praise your dog enthusiastically as he walks beside you. At this early stage of his training, it is permissible for him to walk a foot or two ahead of you, so you can keep the leash slack.

But what happens when he tries to run ahead? Do not give in to the temptation to pull him back. Instead, let the leash pay out, and as it does, grasp the end of the leash in both hands in the proper position for performing the corrective jerk. Stop, and when your dog gets to the end of the six-foot leash, make a ninety-degree turn to the right and jerk the leash sharply to the right with a stern "No!" Your dog has no choice but to stop.

Immediately after this correction, make another ninety-degree turn to the right and start walking briskly in the opposite direction. Whether he wants to or not, your dog will turn and follow you. Pat your

Figures 10, 11, 12, 13, 14, 15. "Heel" training (if dog runs ahead): Dog in starting position alongside trainer; step off with left foot while giving dog verbal command to "Heel"; let dog run ahead to full length of leash; make sharp right turn, jerking leash to the right while repeating verbal command; dog swings around to view trainer; pull in slack while repeating "Heel."

thigh to encourage him to your side. As he draws alongside you, give him an enthusiastic "Good boy!" Gather up three feet of the leash once again and tell him "Oliver, heel."

Do not be surprised if he runs up to you and continues past. Be ready to repeat the entire procedure. Stop and stand perfectly still. Let the leash extend to its full length and grasp it with both hands. The moment he reaches the end of the leash, execute a ninety-degree right turn, jerk the leash sharply to the right, and call out "No!" Make another ninety-degree turn and walk quickly away in the opposite direction. Praise your dog as he hurries to catch up to you. Pat your thigh encouragingly. When he reaches your side, tell him "Oliver, heel."

You may have to repeat this procedure several times. Eventually, your dog will run forward and, anticipating a correction, stop abruptly before he reaches the end of the leash. He is apt to turn his head in your direction to see what you are planning to do.

When he stops on his own, do not correct him. Tell him "Good boy!" pat your thigh to encourage him back to your side, and say, "Oliver, heel." Walk quickly away to the right. Shorten the leash as he draws close to you, and repeat the command: "Oliver, heel."

It is important to keep adjusting the length of the leash. Each time your dog runs ahead, let the leash extend to its full six feet. Each time he hurries back in your direction, gather up half the leash in your right hand once again. Note: If your dog is shy or very small, keep your corrections gentle. A quick tug on the leash is all that's necessary. It is better to err on the side of undercorrecting your dog. You can then increase the strength of your corrections as the training proceeds.

Stay with this exercise until he regularly main-

tains a position no more than one or two feet ahead
of you.

STEP TWO: VARY YOUR PACE AND YOUR DIRECTION

Start this step with a repetition of the last. Walk
back and forth in your practice area at a steady, even
pace. So long as he runs no more than one or two feet
ahead, praise him and keep moving.

Vary your walk. Accelerate as you walk in one
direction and slow down as you head back in the
other. Turn to the left, walk a dozen steps, then turn
to the right and continue on.

You want your dog to keep his attention constantly on you. He must follow you as you take off in
different directions. He must vary his gait to keep
pace with you at all times.

Do not conform to any set pattern. Otherwise your
dog will quickly understand that when you reach
this bench, you always speed up, or when you arrive
at *this* tree, you always turn to the left. He will
respond by memory, and not necessarily by paying
attention.

Throughout these maneuvers, your dog should remain no more than one or two feet away from you. If
he wanders farther from your side, be ready to correct him. Praise him when he resumes walking at
your side.

Stay with this exercise until he follows you,
without error, throughout a full training session.

STEP THREE: OTHER HEELING PROBLEMS

While running ahead is the most common
problem in teaching your dog to "Heel," other difficulties occasionally crop up.

81

Figures 16, 17, 18. "Heel" training (if dog lags behind): Give him physical and verbal encouragement; if dog verges inward, apply left knee; execute right turn.

Figures 19, 20. Automatic "Sit": Slow pace and stop, lower leash and give voice command to "Sit."

STEP FIVE: AUTOMATIC "SIT"

Your dog stays with you now as you walk up and down the street. Your next step is to teach him to stop when you stop and to go instantly into the "Sit" position. This is the automatic "Sit."

You want him to "Sit" when you stop at a corner to wait for the light to change. You want him to "Sit" while you window shop or chat with a friend.

Go back to your practice area. Give him the command "Oliver, heel," and start on a brisk walk. After a minute or so, begin to slow down. Your dog will slow down with you.

Come to a complete halt and tell him to "Sit." Since he already understands the command, he may drop immediately into the "Sit'" position. Praise him.

But if he hesitates, be ready to employ the "Sit" technique. Shorten the leash to roughly eighteen inches. Press down on his haunches with your left hand and, with your right, pull the leash up high and taut. At the same moment, tell him "Sit." Praise him when he responds.

Resume your walk. Take a dozen or more rapid steps, slow down, and come to a halt. Tell your dog to "Sit," press down on his haunches, and pull up on the leash.

It will not take him long to understand what he must do. Slowing your steps alerts him that you are going to stop. In time, he will drop into the "Sit" position on his own, the moment you come to a halt.

STEP SIX: PERFECTING THE "HEEL"

Up to now your dog has been carrying out the "Heel" command by staying within one or two feet

of your thigh. Now you must perfect his performance. To "Heel" properly, he should walk close to
your side with his head *next* to your left thigh.

Go back to your practice area. Stand on the dog's
right and gather up three feet of the leash. Tell him
"Oliver, heel," and step forward on your left foot.

As long as his head remains immediately next to
your thigh, praise him warmly. The moment he
moves ahead, use the corrective technique. Grasp the
three-foot leash (do *not* let it pay out) with both
hands. Jerk it sharply to the right and say "No!" At
the same moment, execute a ninety-degree turn to
the right. When he returns to your side, praise him.

Do not allow any exceptions. Each and every time
his nose moves ahead of your thigh, jerk the leash,
say "No!" and turn right.

Continue to return to your practice area until he
performs without error and it is no longer necessary
to correct him.

16

"Down - Stay"

THE MOMENT you sit down to dinner, your devoted dog gallops into the dining room and skids to a stop alongside your chair. He stares up intently as you lift the first forkful of food to your mouth. His nostrils quiver with anticipation as he watches you swallow and chew. He paws your leg or your chair.

Or say you are comfortably settled in your favorite armchair and your dog is sitting nearby, itching to climb aboard.

How do you settle your dog to keep him from running up to you at the table, or simply so that he can stay without bothering you? You teach him the command "Down."

In the "Down" position, your dog is completely at rest. His entire torso is on the floor, and only his head remains erect. Your dog chooses the "Down" position when he is weary. Following his master from room to room, watching the children play jacks, slurping the water in his dish—such activities tire him and he needs to rest. He flops into the

"Down" position. "Down" is a comfortable position for your dog and, unlike "Sit," one he can remain in indefinitely.

Now you are going to teach him to drop into the "Down" position at your command. And you will teach him to remain in this position—to "Stay" —until you give him permission to move.

Step One: "Down"— The Paw Method at the Dog's Side

Attach the dog's collar and leash and go back to the quiet room you have chosen for your practice sessions. Stand to the right of the dog so that both of you are facing in the same direction.

Gather up four feet of the leash in your right hand. The rest should stretch across your body in a straight line between the dog's collar and your right hand. Tell your dog to "Sit." Praise him when he responds.

Kneel on your left knee, then call out the command "Down." Say only "Down." Keep your tone soft and soothing and draw out the command: "Do-o-w-w-n." At the same moment, with your left hand pull the dog's front paws forward. Do it gently. Be certain to pull both paws at the same time. To avoid squeezing the dog's paws together, which can be painful for him, keep one finger between them.

Pulling his paws forward will bring his body to the ground. Throughout this procedure, maintain leash control.

Your dog may resist being pushed into this position. If you are practicing in a carpeted room, he may dig his paws into the floor and refuse to budge. In that case, shift to a room without carpeting. It will be easier to slide his paws forward on a smooth floor.

Once he is settled into the "Down" position,

89

praise him. It does not matter that you maneuvered him into it. His torso is on the floor, his head is high; he is obeying your command. Praise him!

Put him back in the "Sit" position and repeat the exercise until he drops into the "Down" position without resistance.

STEP TWO: "DOWN"— THE PAW METHOD IN FRONT OF THE DOG

You are going to guide your dog into the "Down" position while kneeling in front of him. Your aim is to condition the dog to follow your command while he is able to see you.

Start by standing on the right side of the dog. Put him in "Sit-Stay," step forward and to the left with your right foot, and execute an about-face. You are now standing directly in front of your dog.

Kneel on either knee. In this position, with eye-to-eye contact established, your dog may take it into his head that you want to play. He may try to leap forward. It is essential that you control him with the leash.

With your left hand, grasp the leash about one and a half feet from the dog's collar and hold it high and taut above the dog's head. This will prevent him from moving forward. Be certain to hold the leash to the side so that it doesn't hit his chin.

Call out the command "Down." Keep your tone soft and encouraging. At the same moment, grasp the dog's forepaws with your right hand and gently pull them forward.

Since this is not a new position for your dog, he will probably offer little resistance. When his torso reaches the floor, praise him warmly. Repeat this exercise at least a dozen times. Remember, the key to successful training is constant repetition.

Step Three: "Down"—
The Hand Method at the Dog's Side

In this step, we introduce a hand signal. Since some dogs are hand shy and may flinch or nip if a hand comes down in front of them, it is important to start by working at the side of your dog.

Stand to the right of the dog and put him in "Sit." Hold the leash high and taut in your right hand. Raise your left hand above the dog's eye level. Keep your fingers extended and your palm flat.

Call out the command "Down." At the same moment, slowly lower your left hand. As your palm

Figure 21. "Down"—the paw method (especially suited for small dogs): Start with left hand placed between dog's two front paws while giving verbal command "Down."

Figures 22, 23, 24, 25.
"Down"—the hand method:
With left hand above dog,
give verbal command
"Down"; lower left hand
and press down where leash
meets collar; bend left knee
while applying downward
pressure; final position with
dog resting on ground.

reaches the level of the dog's neck, press down on the leash at the point where it meets the dog's collar. The pressure of your palm moving downward on the leash will force the dog's torso to the floor. Note: If your dog is oversized or powerfully built, the pressure of your palm may not be enough. In this case, put your left elbow on the back of his neck as your palm reaches the leash. Use the full weight of your arm, from elbow to palm, to force your dog down. Or, if even that isn't enough, use your left foot as in figures 26 and 27.

Out of the corner of his eye, the dog observes your hand slowly lowering to the floor. As you repeat this exercise, he comes to associate this signal—your hand descending—with the verbal command "Down."

Repeat this exercise a dozen times. Do not be discouraged if your pet doesn't get the hang of it in one session. This is a hard lesson for him to learn. Stay calm and keep your tone cheerful. Eventually, you will find that he slips into the "Down" position without the pressure of your palm on the leash. At that point, move on to the next step.

STEP FOUR: "DOWN"—THE HAND METHOD
KNEELING IN FRONT OF THE DOG

You are going to guide the dog into the "Down" position using the same hand-on-leash method as in the last step. But you are going to do it while kneeling in front of the dog.

This is important. You want the dog to see your descending hand movement fully and clearly. This strengthens his association of your hand signal with your vocal command. Eventually either the signal or the command—by itself—will suffice.

Figures 26, 27. *"Down"—sliding-leash technique for stubborn or aggressive dogs: Secure leash under foot, then pull upward on leash while giving vocal command "Down"; for larger dogs, slide foot upward so that dog is forced down.*

Since he has already been exposed to your hand falling at his side, he is now ready to accept—without fear—your hand descending in front of him. (And you can feel secure that he will not try to nip you.)

Place him in "Sit-Stay," step off on your right foot, execute an about-face, and stand before him. Kneel on either knee. Hold the leash high and taut in your left hand. Raise your right hand above his head, pointing up and with the palm flat and fingers extended and joined.

Call out the command "Do-o-w-w-n." At the same time, slowly lower your right hand. With your flattened palm, press down on the leash at the point

95

where it meets the collar until both the leash and the dog's torso have reached the floor. Congratulate him.

Since he is now familiar with the palm-pressing-down-on-the-leash technique from the previous steps, chances are he will drop into the "Down" position willingly. However, do not shortchange his practice. Repeat the exercise a dozen times. Remember to praise him after each successful effort.

STEP FIVE: THE HAND METHOD STANDING IN FRONT OF THE DOG

Place the dog in "Sit-Stay" and execute an about-face so that you stand in front of him. Hold the leash high and taut in one hand. Raise your other hand, fingers straight up and close together.

Call out the command "Do-o-w-w-n." Use a soft, encouraging tone. At the same moment, swing your hand down and to your side, letting it brush lightly against the leash. Remain standing and do not force the leash to the floor.

If your dog has absorbed his lessons to this point, chances are he will drop into the "Down" position by himself. Give him lots of praise when he does.

Repeat the exercise a dozen times. Then move back until you are standing roughly three feet in front of him. Raise your hand, fingers stretched upward. Slowly lower your hand to your side as you draw out the command "Do-o-w-w-n." Do not touch the leash. By the time your hand returns to your side,

Figures 28, 29, 30. "Down" from a distance of six feet: With dog at end of six-foot leash, raise right hand; dog begins to go down as right hand is lowered to side; command completed.

your dog should be in the "Down" position. Let him know what a smart fellow he is!

Drill him until he responds perfectly at least a dozen times in a row. Then move back the full length of the six-foot leash and perform the same exercise from there.

STEP SIX: "DOWN-STAY"

Now that your dog understands "Down," the next step is to teach him to remain in the "Down" position—to "Stay"—until you release him from the command. You follow the same technique you used for "Sit-Stay."

Take him through the last step. Stand in front of him, lower your hand, and give him the command "Down." Praise him when he complies. Tell him to "Stay" and back away the full length of the six-foot leash. "Atta boy!"

Holding the leash high and taut, move several feet to the left. He hasn't budged. Stop and congratulate him. Reverse your direction and move several feet to the right. "Smart fellow!"

Walk a full circle around him. Call out "Stay" at various points along your path.

Since your dog already understands "Sit-Stay," this will be an easy lesson for him. Nevertheless, stay with this exercise until you are able to circle him—while he remains in place—at least half a dozen times in a row. Praise him and call it a day.

STEP SEVEN: "DOWN-STAY" WITHOUT THE LEASH, INDOORS

Go back to your training area and attach the dog's collar and leash. Put your dog in "Down-Stay" and walk back to the end of the six-foot leash. Praise him.

Drop your end of the leash to the floor. Tell him "Stay." Keeping your hands at your sides, walk a full circle around him.

With his "Sit-Stay" training solidly behind him, he will no doubt remain in place. Tell him what a smart fellow he is, remind him once again to "Stay," and walk out of the room. Return in several seconds and congratulate him.

Gradually increase the length of time until you are able to remain out of the room for a full ten minutes. Remember, "Down" is a comfortable position for your dog, one that he can remain in indefinitely.

STEP EIGHT: PRACTICAL APPLICATION
WITHOUT THE LEASH, INDOORS

Now that he responds to "Down-Stay" without any leash control in his training sessions, it is time to put his training to practical use. Your ultimate aim is to have him respond to the command while he is running loose, with his leash off, throughout the house.

There will be times when you want him to remain in one spot for some ten minutes or more. Perhaps you want to ring up a friend and have a long and undisturbed chat. Or you want to concentrate on balancing your checkbook. Great. Lower your hand to signal him into "Down-Stay."

This practical application in addition to his formal training sessions will shorten the time it takes him to learn the command and understand fully that he must follow it under all circumstances, all the time.

17

"Come When Called"

Your KITCHEN floor has just been waxed and you want your dog to stay off it. "Come over here this minute," you call to him. He doesn't come.

The electrician is repairing an outlet in your den and the wires are exposed. "Come here before you get hurt," you cry out. The dog ignores your command.

Your daughter's homework lies untouched while she romps with the dog. "No playing now," you order. "Come here, King." King behaves as if he never heard you.

Time and again throughout the day, you call your dog to come to you. You plead, you shout, you scold. Nothing works; he never responds.

You are at your wit's end. It is time to teach your dog the command "Come When Called." In this command, you teach your dog to respond immediately to your call. He must stop whatever he is doing, run directly to you, and drop into the "Sit" position in front of you.

You will be competing for his attention with all the temptations in your house, so praise takes on a special importance. Each time he responds to your call, give him total, enthusiastic praise. Such praise will motivate him to drop what he is doing and run to your side. He must be convinced that the welcome that awaits him is far more exhilarating than any activity he is leaving behind.

Your dog may refuse to answer your call because he associates it with scolding and punishment. If your dog misbehaves and it is necessary to correct him, *do not call him to your side. Go to him for any correction.* Coming to you should be a happy experience at all times. Never call him in order to chastise him. He will very quickly lose interest in answering your call. Remember, if he needs correction, go to him; when he answers your call and comes to you, greet him with praise.

In this command, we use three words: "Okay, [Name], come."

We have already discussed the use of "Okay" as a release from a command position. "Okay" also has a second use: It sets the mood of a command. It is always delivered in a light, cheerful tone and suggests to your dog that something exciting is in store for him. It alerts him to pay attention. It is in this sense that we use "Okay" in this command.

The second word—your dog's name—is used in all forward-action commands. It is a signal to the dog to get ready to move forward.

The third word—"Come"—tells him what he must do.

These are the words that you use in calling your dog. Once he is trained, continue to use them. Do not call him to you in any other way. Alert the rest of the family to do the same.

STEP ONE: COMING TO YOU

Go back to the quiet room you have chosen for your practice sessions.

Attach his collar and leash and stand on his right side. Tell him to "Sit" and then "Stay." Back away to the end of the six-foot leash.

Stand facing the dog and hold the leash high in your left hand. Allow some slack in the leash so that you do not pull the dog forward.

Let's say your dog's name is Rusty. Teaching this command requires that you do three things simultaneously. First, call out "Okay, Rusty, come." Put your emphasis on the word "Okay" so that it sounds like "Oka-a-ay, Rusty, come." Use a cheerful, encouraging tone. You want your words to entice your dog to come running to you.

Second, as you say the word "Okay," tug gently on the leash. This reinforces your dog's understanding of what he is supposed to do.

Third, also on the word "Okay," use your right hand to execute the kind of hand signal you use to beckon someone to you. From a slightly raised, extended position—palm flat, fingers together—swing it quickly toward your chest.

The complete command becomes "Oka-a-ay [pull forward on the leash; beckon with your right hand], Rusty, come."

Continue to hold your left hand high as your dog comes running to you. This will insure that his paws do not get tangled in the leash.

The moment he reaches you, praise him exuberantly. It does not matter if he jumps up and down before you with excitement, or if he doesn't arrive exactly in front of you. At this early stage of his training, all that matters is that he respond to your command. You call him, he comes. Lavish him with praise.

Repeat the procedure. Put him in "Sit-Stay" and stand six feet in front of him. Hold the leash high—and a little slack—in your left hand. Call out "Okay, Rusty, come." On the word "Okay," pull forward on the leash and use your right hand to beckon him. "Terrific! Smart fellow!"

Practice this exercise a dozen times. You want your dog to become familiar with the words and to recognize the hand signal. The hand signal will prove especially important later, when he is off his leash. He must learn to "see" as well as "hear" your command.

Encourage him to respond immediately. Work with him until he learns to rise and take off the moment he hears that first word, "Okay." This may require several practice sessions.

When he performs consistently and with speed, move on to the next step.

STEP TWO: SITTING BEFORE YOU

Put your dog in "Sit-Stay" and back away the full length of the six-foot leash. Hold the leash high in your left hand, allowing a bit of slack.

In your most exuberant tone, call out "Oka-a-ay, Rusty, come."

It should no longer be necessary to tug on the leash. Your dog understands that he must rise and run to you. It is important, however, to use the hand signal. At the moment you say "Okay," beckon him to you.

Figures 31, 32, 33, 34.
"Come": Hand signal begins
with simultaneous voice
command; hand signal com-
pleted, right hand grasps
leash . . .

. . . Leash is reeled in as dog comes; command completed.

Immediately after you signal him, move your right hand to the leash and use both hands, in a one-over-one method, to reel in the leash like a fishing line. By the time your dog reaches your feet, all but one foot of leash should be gathered up.

Hold the one foot of leash high and taut in your left hand. Tell your dog to "Sit," pulling upward on the leash to guide him into the "Sit" position. Shower him with praise.

The importance of "Sitting" becomes apparent when your dog is off his leash and is coming at you from across a long room. If he is running at great speed, he may not be able to stop in time and will continue to run past you. Or he may, like a bull, charge directly into you. This may not seem significant if you own a Chihuahua, but it can be disastrous if your dog is a Mastiff or a St. Bernard.

Having to "Sit" compels him to slow his pace before he reaches you.

It does not matter that you maneuvered him into the "Sit" position by pulling up on the leash. Be lavish in your praise. This is a complicated lesson for your dog to learn. It requires that he perform two separate actions. First, he must run forward the moment you call him. Second, he must drop into the "Sit" position as he arrives at your feet.

Repeat the procedure. Stand six feet in front of your dog and call out "Okay, Rusty, come." On the word "Okay," beckon him with your right hand. Then, using both hands, reel in all but one foot of the leash as your dog comes running to you. Hold the leash high and taut above his head and tell him to "Sit." Praise him.

After several repetitions you will find it no longer necessary to pull up on the leash. He will automatically slow his steps as he nears you and, on his own, drop into the "Sit" position. Praise him well.

Stay with this exercise until he performs it correctly at least a dozen times in a row.

STEP THREE: PRACTICAL APPLICATION WITH THE LEASH ON

Your dog responds accurately to your command within the controlled situation of the training session. Now you must put his training to practical use.

Attach his collar and leash, walk him into the living room, and tell him to "Sit." Ask a friend or family member to stand nearby and bounce a ball.

Allow your dog a minute or two to watch this fascinating exhibition. Then, putting as much good cheer into your voice as you can, call out "Okay, Rusty, come."

He may rise immediately, run to you, and sit at your feet. If so, go all out in your praise. He has learned his lessons well.

But it is far more likely that he will cast a fleeting glance in your direction and then turn his attention back to the bouncing ball.

He has disobeyed you; you must correct him.

Grasp the leash in both hands and jerk it sharply to the right. At the same moment, call out a stern and disapproving "No!" Then, shift your voice back to cheerfulness and tell him "Okay, Rusty, come." When he arrives at your feet, let him know how wise and obedient he is.

Repeat this procedure on successive days. You may employ different means to distract him. What is important is that his attention be elsewhere when you call him to come.

When he responds consistently despite a variety of distractions, move on to the next step.

Step Four: Dropping the Leash

Your ultimate goal is to have your dog respond to your call while he is running loose in the house. In this step you will teach him to obey your command with his leash off.

Attach his collar and leash and go back to your training room. Tell your dog to "Sit." Back away to the end of the leash and call out "Okay, Rusty, come." Beckon him with your arm and reel in the leash. When he stops and sits in front of you, praise him.

Now, remove the leash and lay it out flat on the floor, fully extended to its six-foot length and slightly to one side. You do not want the dog to trip over it when he comes running to you.

Although the leash is no longer on him, your dog is able to see it in front of him. Psychologically, he is still very aware of the leash.

Stand six feet in front of him and call out "Okay, Rusty, come." At the same moment, beckon him with your right arm.

He should respond exactly as he does when the leash is attached. He must rise and run to you immediately and sit automatically in front of your feet. Give him enthusiastic praise.

If your dog does not obey, it will be necessary to go back one step and work with him again while his leash is on. Reinforce his understanding of the command with additional practice on the leash. Do not lose patience. Remember, it takes repetition to get successful results.

Repeat this exercise, standing six feet in front of your dog, while the leash lies flat on the floor. When he responds correctly, praise him and move back two more feet. Practice the exercise at this eight-foot distance at least half a dozen times.

Continue to work your way back slowly, two feet at a time, until you are calling to him across the length of the room. Throughout the session, keep the leash on the floor, in front of your dog. Praise him each and every time he responds correctly.

STEP FIVE: PRACTICAL APPLICATION WITH THE LEASH OFF

Now that your dog responds without a leash in his training sessions, do not hesitate to put this training into practice. Use it freely throughout the day while he is roaming untethered around the house.

Remember always to call to him in a cheerful tone. In that way, your dog will enjoy answering your call.

You will quickly discover that this is one command you cannot do without.

IV

Off-Leash Training

18

INTRODUCTION

A FAMILIAR outdoor scene depicts a dog sprinting through the park or down the road with his master in hot pursuit. The master is flailing his arms and shouting something like "Barnaby, come back! This instant!" His face is red, his tone is angry, and he is obviously out of breath.

And Barnaby? He's having a wonderful time! There is nothing as exhilarating as a game of "chase me" with his master.

The master wonders why his dog doesn't obey. After all, isn't Barnaby housebroken? Isn't he a model of good behavior in the house? And doesn't Barnaby walk by his side on a leash?

The last is a common misconception among dog owners. They assume that the dog who obeys on a leash will also obey when his leash is off. They take for granted that the dog who "behaves" in the house will also behave when turned loose outdoors.

A dog's understanding is limited by the extent of his training. His basic training taught him to follow your commands while you were hanging on to the end of the leash. If you want him to do your bidding outdoors while you are physically separated from him, if you want him to heed your calls from a considerable distance, if you want him to respond despite the turmoil and temptations in any area, then you must teach him the off-leash commands.

Off-leash training cannot be started until the dog has completed his basic training. The off-leash course requires a half hour of daily training for a period of four to six months. The length of time depends on your dog's breed and temperament.

As a rule, the dog that is "people oriented" learns faster. He is eager to please his master, he pays attention, and he tries hard. The Standard Poodle, the German Shepherd, and the Doberman Pinscher are prime examples.

At the other end of the scale are the hunting dogs. The Weimaraner's sense of adventure, the Irish Setter's desire to roam, and the Labrador Retriever's need to explore make it difficult for these breeds to sit in class and concentrate.

But within breeds, temperament plays a key role. The responsive dog of any breed makes a better student than a stubborn or strong-willed dog.

Once your dog completes his training, do you place any limits on his freedom? Obviously, it would be folly to allow your dog to roam off leash near a crowded intersection at the height of rush-hour traffic. You can, however, give him total freedom in an enclosed playground or park. Most trained dogs are trustworthy when turned loose in an open suburban area, and some dogs honor their training on a quiet city street. How much freedom you give your dog depends on his temperament, his intelligence, and his breed (you should, of course, be aware of your local leash laws and act accordingly). In the final analysis, it is a decision only you can make.

Throughout this book, simply as a matter of convenience, I have been referring to your dog as "he." Actually, in some breeds the male requires more time and effort to train off leash. He may be a fighter, or wanderlust may be in his blood. The female of such breeds, generally less aggressive and more of a homebody, makes a better candidate for off-leash training. The last part of this book distinguishes these breeds.

Training Tools

For off-leash training you will need several pieces of equipment in addition to the choke collar and the standard six-foot leash. Three of these were

Figure 35. Off-leash equipment: six-foot leash, handle.

described in chapter 2 and were used in the advanced stages of basic obedience training: *a clothesline* (for off leash, a minimum of twenty feet), a *fishline,* and a *throw chain.* There is one other item essential to off-leash training: a *leash handle.*

This is the hand loop at the end of the leash, which in most cases is either sewn or snap-fastened to the body of the leash, combined with the clip from the other end. For off-leash training, the handle from an extralightweight leash serves best. Remove handle and clip from the body of the leash and attach them to give yourself a control piece approximately six inches long. An alternative is to fold and wrap a full leash securely to the same length (see figure 35).

19

THE "HEEL"

LEARNING TO "HEEL" on leash was a huge accomplishment for your dog. He learned to walk on your left side, at your pace, with his head close to your thigh. He learned to match his gait to yours, whether you were doing a slow shuffle down the block or striding purposefully with giant-size steps. He will now stop when you stop, "Sit" automatically by your side, and rise to his feet and start to walk again at the exact moment you do. He can execute left turns and right turns and about-face, following your movements with the precision of a Radio City Rockette.

All this is against your dog's natural inclination. Actually, he'd like to move at his own pace, in double-quick time when he spots another dog at the end of the block, or slow almost to a halt as he passes some children at play. But he has learned to curb his instincts and give full attention to you.

Your dog may believe that he "Heels" solely to please you and to earn your praise, but let's face it, he is also aware of the collar around his neck and the leash you hold in your hand. If he's honest with himself he'll admit that he really has no choice but to "Heel."

In teaching him to "Heel" off leash, you must convince him that he still has no choice. Of course you will be pleased and of course you will praise him. But let him make no mistake about it, at the end of his training, with his leash removed, he will have no more doubt about "Heeling" than he had when trained on leash.

For your first training session, select an enclosed and quiet area. You need the dog's undivided attention and you want to keep outside distractions to a minimum. In the suburbs, an enclosed backyard is fine. So is the basement of your house. In the city, you may step out of your apartment and take advantage of the long hallway during the quiet hours of the day, or select a schoolyard or secluded park area.

Do not feed him before a training session—his mind might wander to thoughts of a siesta. Be certain that he relieves himself before you begin.

Start his training by reviewing his "Heeling" on leash. With his leash and collar attached, stand to his right and tell him to "Sit." The well-trained dog will immediately squat on your left side. Use only the word "Sit." Do not preface the command with his name. In his on-leash training your dog learned to associate the sound of his name with a call to forward action. It means "on your mark, get ready, get set—."

Let's say that your dog's name is Charlie. Now that he is in the proper "Sitting" position, give him the action command. Tell him, "Charlie, heel!" At the same moment, tap him gently behind the ear with the fingertips of your left hand and move forward on your left foot.

Your dog will rise and move forward, too. Walk

about ten or fifteen steps and slow to a stop. Your dog will stop and "Sit." This is all old hat to him.

Walk back and forth, stopping and then starting up again. Vary the pace of your walk. Turn to the left and then to the right. At all times, your dog's head should be parallel to your left thigh and his movement should synchronize perfectly with yours.

After several minutes, your dog will no doubt raise his forepaw to stifle a yawn. At this point it is time to begin his training off leash.

STEP ONE: DRAPE THE LEASH AROUND YOUR NECK

Put the dog in a "Sit" position at your left. Take your end of the leash and drape it around the back of your neck. The leash handle will dangle in front of you, on your right side (see figure 37). Let your hands hang free at your sides. If you are working with a small dog, it may be necessary to use a longer or double leash.

While he "Sits," call out the command, "Charlie, heel." At the same moment, nudge him behind the ear and step forward. Be certain to start with your left foot. This is the foot that is closest to his head and he will have no difficulty seeing you take this first step.

If he is confused because he cannot see the leash in your hand, he may not move. Be prepared to correct him. With your left hand, reach for the leash where it meets his collar, jerk it firmly, and say "No!"

Repeat your command, "Charlie, heel." Once again tap him behind the ear and step forward with your left foot. He will soon recognize that this is, after all, the same old "Heel" command, and will fall into step with you.

Walk forward ten or fifteen steps at a steady, even

Figures 36, 37, 38, 39.
"Heel": With leash draped
around your neck, give dog
simultaneous voice and
hand commands to "Heel";
dog begins to obey; right
turn—jerk leash to the right
with left hand while giving
verbal command to "Heel";
left turn—pull leash back
and to the left, and place
right foot in front of dog.

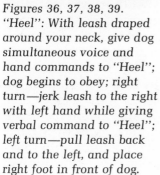

pace, congratulating him on his performance. Come to a slow halt and allow him to "Sit." If he fails to "Sit" automatically, reach for the leash, correct him, and say "No." Then tell him to "Sit." Praise him when he does.

After a moment's rest, repeat the procedure. Give the vocal command, "Charlie, heel," tap him behind the ear, and step forward on your left foot. Walk fifteen steps and come to a halt. Praise him when he "Sits."

The session should last roughly fifteen minutes. Each time he performs correctly, let him know how smart he is. Plan two fifteen-minute sessions each day.

When he is "Heeling" and "Sitting" without error as you walk steadily forward, start to vary your tempo and direction. Introduce left and right turns. Accelerate your speed as you walk in one direction and slow down as you turn in another. At all times, his head should remain parallel to your left thigh.

As you vary your walk, a number of errors may creep into his performance. Reach for the leash immediately. You cannot allow him to get too far out of line or the leash will slip from your neck.

If your dog forges ahead: Pull sharply on the leash, tell him "No," and execute a quick, right turn. Your dog will skid to a stop and have no choice but to reverse his steps and sprint after you. Pat your thigh to encourage him. Praise him when he catches up.

This correction is a jarring experience for your dog. It will alert him to keep his attention fixed on you. Your praise will reassure him that he is behaving properly when he walks by your side.

If he lags behind: Execute a quick pull forward on the leash, call out "No," and take several brisk steps forward. This will jolt him out of his lethargy and send him scurrying to close the gap between you. Pat your thigh to encourage his joining you and give him praise. Note: If your dog is shy, patting your thigh to encourage may be enough.

If he widens the gap between you: Tug the leash sharply to the right and tell him "No." Pat your thigh and urge him back to your side with a "C'mon, boy!" Be sure to praise him.

If he narrows the gap between you: He may begin to walk inward, stepping in front of your path. To avoid a head-over-heels disaster, pull the leash backward and tell him "No!" Use your left knee to guide him into the proper position. Praise him.

If he fails to follow you in a right turn: Employ the same technique you use when he lags behind. Jerk the leash quickly, call out "No!" and execute another right turn. Walk on briskly. Coax him to your side and give him praise.

If he fails to follow you in a left turn: Jerk the leash to the right and tell him "No." Coax him by patting your thigh and quickening your pace. When he catches up to you, tell him how smart he is.

Practice for fifteen minutes at a time and hold two sessions a day. Stay with this exercise for one week, or until your dog turns in a perfect fifteen-minute performance.

STEP TWO: REMOVE THE LEASH
AND USE THE HANDLE AND FISHLINE

Go back to the quiet area you have chosen. Your dog will begin to identify this area as his campus and will understand that it is time to attend his class. Bring along a twelve-foot length of fishline and a pair of heavy gloves.

Review step one. With his leash and collar attached, drape the leash around your neck. Call out

"Charlie, heel," tap him behind his ear, and move forward on your left foot. Walk swiftly for a dozen steps, slow down to a leisurely pace for a dozen more, then shift gears once again into a normal, steady gait. He should turn in an A performance.

Now remove the leash from your dog's collar. Detach the handle from the leash, and clip the *handle only* to the collar. Thread the short fishline through the handle, and hold on to both ends of the line in your right hand. Hold the line taut so that the leash handle stands out horizontally from the dog's collar (see figure 40).

Slip on your gloves. If you have to deliver a correction, the gloves will prevent the line from cutting into your hands.

Figure 40. Walking dog with short fishline attached to handle.

Note: The fishline, unlike the body of the leash, is weightless and almost invisible. Your dog will be unaware of its presence.

In the first step, with the leash lying across your shoulders, your dog no longer saw the leash. Now, with the body of the leash off, he no longer feels its full weight. He is another step closer to freedom.

He may get the notion that school is over for the day. While he sits pondering this delicious possibility, call out "Charlie, heel," tap him behind the ear, and step forward on your left foot.

If Charlie has been dreaming of going home, he may not move forward with you. Pull sharply on the fishline and tell him "No."

It may come as a shock to your dog that, with the

Figure 41. Fishline removed, dog walking off leash.

Figures 42, 43. "Heel," with
leash handle only: Review
command with handle but
no leash; maintain only
light control on handle.

leash off, you are able to deliver a correction. He will quickly fall into line. Congratulate him for displaying such good sense. Then repeat "Charlie, heel," tap him gently behind the ear, and step forward again on your left foot.

Walk leisurely for some fifteen steps, then turn to the left. Accelerate your gait for another fifteen steps, and turn to the right. Continue the exercise, varying your direction and pace.

If he falters at any point, be ready to correct him. Pull sharply on the fishline and tell him "No." Employ the techniques given in step one. Work at this exercise for fifteen minutes at a time and hold two sessions a day.

When you are satisfied with his performance, get ready to retire the fishline. As your dog walks in "Heel," drop one end of the line to the ground. The leash handle will slip from its taut horizontal position and dangle loosely from your dog's collar (see figure 41).

Continue walking as if nothing has changed. Of course you are aware that holding on to one end of the fishline is useless, that you cannot jerk the line and deliver a correction. But your dog doesn't know this. Remain calm and confident. Take firm, deliberate steps as you walk back and forth and make your turns.

Keep in mind that there is an alternate means of physical correction available to you. If your dog's performance becomes sloppy, reach for the leash handle with your left hand and pull it quickly and sharply to the right. At this stage, however, your dog is probably so well trained that very little if any physical correction should be necessary.

If he maintains his excellent performance, discard the fishline. In future sessions, work with the leash handle only.

Remain with this step for about a week. Your dog's breed and temperament will determine how long it takes him to absorb this exercise fully.

STEP THREE: PRACTICE FIGURE EIGHTS

Be certain that your dog has an empty stomach and that he has relieved himself before the session begins. And if you tend to seasickness or are susceptible to vertigo, it is a good idea, for this figure-eight exercise, that your stomach be empty, too.

Bring two folding chairs to your practice area and set them up roughly ten feet apart. Attach the leash handle to the dog's collar and position yourself and the dog midway between the chairs.

Start off with the command, "Charlie, heel," tap him behind the ear, and step forward with your left foot. Move diagonally to the right, circle the first chair, continue to the left and circle the other. When you have completed a full figure eight, return to your original position and come to a halt.

If your dog is puzzled by this new routine and fails to "Heel" properly, reach down for the handle, administer a correction, and tell him "No." Then repeat the command "Charlie, heel." When he steps into line, walking close to your left thigh, be sure to praise him.

In this step, your dog is learning a variety of maneuvers. He is "Heeling" without his leash as you move in to the left or away to the right. He follows you around in circles. To perform correctly, his eyes must be riveted to your left leg and his full concentration must be on the movement of your feet.

At first, practice the figure eight in the same direction at a steady, measured pace. Give him time to accustom himself to the pattern. Slow down to a halt each time you return to your starting position. Praise him enthusiastically with each correct figure eight. Work at it for fifteen minutes at a time, and hold two sessions a day.

When he is perfect in this standard figure eight, vary the drill. Sometimes lead off to the left, sometimes to the right. Vary your pace. Walk slowly to the right of the chair, accelerate into a trot as you circle the chair, and reduce your speed to a normal gait as you head the other way. Stop and have your dog "Sit" at different points along the way.

If at any point in your circling he stops to examine and sniff the chairs, reach for the handle, deliver a

Figures 44, 45. "Heel," completely off leash.

firm correction, and give him a stern "No." Then praise him and command him to "Heel" once again. Your dog will learn that no matter what distraction is nearby, he must concentrate solely on you.

When his performance is consistently correct, pack away the folding chairs and go on to the next step.

STEP FOUR: FIGURE EIGHTS WITH TWO ASSISTANTS

Enlist the aid of two friends or members of the family. Ask them to join you in your practice area and have them stand ten feet apart. Position yourself midway between them with your dog seated by your left side. Attach the handle of his leash to his collar, then give him the command "Charlie, heel."

If his eyes are focused on one of your assistants and he fails to respond, reach down for the leash handle and execute a correction. In a very stern voice, tell him "No." Then start over. Give the command "Charlie, heel," and when he responds, give him a "Good boy!"

Run him through the figure-eight drills. Start slowly and build up speed. Make wide turns and narrow ones. Alternate your direction.

The presence of the two assistants is a further test of your dog's ability to focus full attention on you. It may not have been too difficult for him to ignore the inanimate chairs; it may be much harder to ignore those two live bipeds who have suddenly joined the class.

But ignore them he must. You are preparing him for the day when you walk outdoors without his leash, through populated areas. He must learn to overlook all distractions and stay glued to your side.

Practice this exercise for at least fifteen minutes, twice a day. Remain with this step for about a week, or until your dog runs through several sessions without error.

STEP FIVE: REMOVE THE HANDLE FROM HIS COLLAR

Go back to your practice area along with your two aides. Attach the handle to your dog's collar and spend several minutes warming up with figure eights. Then remove the handle from the collar.

Stand midway between your two assistants and begin a figure eight. The new feeling of weightlessness between him and you may set off some giddy sensations in your dog. He may forge ahead compulsively or lag behind with a slightly inebriated grin on his face.

You cannot allow his execution to become sloppy. To correct his lagging, do not stop your forward movement. Instead, walk a bit faster. At the same moment, pat your thigh in encouragement and call out his name. This probably will be enough to sober him up and send him scurrying to your side. When he does, give him abundant praise.

If he forges ahead, try the reverse procedure. Slow your pace, pat your thigh, and call out his name. Or stop and make a quick turn to the right. Then pat your thigh and call to him. The realization that he is losing you will no doubt clear his brain. When he rushes to your side, be sure to tell him how smart he is.

If he attempts to move away horizontally, move the entire exercise to a wall or fence or row of shrubs. He'll have no choice but to narrow the gap between you.

And, finally, if he steps into your path, use your knee against his flanks to guide him outward. When he aligns himself properly, congratulate him.

He may need one or two sessions to become accustomed to this new lightweight feeling. When he begins to perform properly, be sure to praise him. Practice this step in fifteen-minute sessions, twice a day.

Step Six: Practical Application

Your dog is now ready to move from the exercises of the classroom to practical application off campus. He is ready to leave his secluded training area and step into the hustle and bustle of the outside world.

Choose a busy park area. Or select an open street (but one with a minimum of traffic). Bring the throw chain with you.

When you arrive at your destination, remove your dog's leash. This is his big moment! Will he take advantage of his untethered state and decide to run for the hills? If he has repeatedly turned in a flawless performance of "Heeling" at your side for several weeks, and if he has been enthusiastically complimented for his fine execution, he won't. But he must respect your authority and understand that you are the boss.

Consider that last sentence. At this crucial point in your dog's training, your attitude becomes most important. Out in the street, with no leash between you and your pet, you may experience a sudden lack of confidence. You may become convinced that you will not be able to control your dog. You may wish you had never thought of training your dog off leash.

Any such message will quickly convey itself to your dog and undo much of the training of the last few weeks. It is absolutely necessary that you do not betray any anxiety. You must maintain an attitude of calm, confident control. Your manner must suggest that you expect nothing less than total obedience from him, with or without physical controls.

Hold in your left hand the leash you have just removed from your dog. His seeing the leash, even though he is well aware it is no longer on him, will serve as a psychological deterrent. Keep the throw chain in your right hand.

With a firm, authoritative voice, call out the command "Charlie, heel." Do not let any hesitation creep into your voice. Do not pose it as a question. Announce it as a simple command. At the same time, tap him gently behind the ear and step forward firmly on your left foot.

Do not let your foot hesitate uncertainly in mid-air. Do not look at your dog expectantly to see if he is going to "Heel." Plant your left foot squarely on the grass or asphalt and assume that your dog will walk by your side.

With your dog off leash, the throw chain is your final instrument of correction. Jiggle it as you set off on your walk. The clinking of the metal simulates the sound of your dog's collar when he is being corrected. It is an aural reminder to the dog that if he does not perform properly, a correction will be on its way.

Start your off-leash walk at a smooth, steady pace. If at any point he lags behind or forges ahead, if he tends to step into your path or veer away from you, jiggle the throw chain and call out "No!" Nothing more should be necessary to get him to step back into line. Praise him and continue your walk. Gradually start to vary your direction and the tempo of your steps.

Walk into as many diversions as are feasible along

the way. Head for a cluster of chattering people, circle a baby carriage, turn to the left and then to the right.

As he follows you through these parade-ground maneuvers, be liberal in your praise. "Good boy!" "What a smart fellow!"

There is always the possibility that a sudden distraction may prove irresistible. Another dog appears and suddenly your well-behaved Charlie emits a low growl and breaks into a run. What do you do?

Toss the throw chain at the ground beside him and shout out a very stern "No!" The clink of the chain and the sound of your voice should bring him to his senses. When he stops, give him enthusiastic praise. Then call out the "Heel" command and start all over.

In time, widen and diversify the areas you choose. Meander along a country road, stride briskly through a quiet city lane, stroll barefoot in the sand. If he follows you faithfully, over sand and asphalt and grass, accept my congratulations. Your dog has passed his "Heeling" off leash.

20

"Sit - Stay"

BETWEEN BURSTS of activity through a normal day, your dog needs to stop every now and then to catch his breath. He "Sits." As he squats on his haunches, his body is at rest but his mind remains alert. He is like a football player temporarily benched from the game. The player's weary arms and legs are grateful for the recess, but his ears remain attentive to the sounds of the game and his eyes are riveted to the action. "Sitting" is the ideal posture for your dog to recharge his physical batteries while still in touch with the passing scene.

In his basic training, your dog learned that he must also "Sit" when it pleases you. And, once "Sitting," that he must remain in that position—he must "Stay"—until you release him from the command.

This has undeniable advantages for you. Your frisky dog will, at your command, "Sit-Stay" while you trim your toenails or pop a contact lens back

Figures 46, 47. Basic "Sit-Stay": Holding leash with dog at side, give hand and voice commands to "Stay"; repeat command with dog at end of six-foot leash.

into place. And he'll "Sit-Stay" in the backyard, watching your youngsters play ball and not try to get into the game himself.

Now you are going to teach him to "Sit-Stay" in public areas, amid distractions and at a considerable distance from you. You will teach him to remain in that position, whether or not he is able to see you, for minutes at a time (though not more than ten minutes, after which the position can get uncomfortable for your dog).

Start his training by reviewing his "Sit-Stays" indoors, with you close by. Choose a quiet room in the house where the two of you can be alone. Attach his collar and leash and hold the leash in your right hand. Position yourself on his right, with your left hand hanging free at your side, and tell him to "Sit."

When he is squatting comfortably, call out the command "Stay." At the same moment, pass your left hand before the dog's eyes. Do not touch his face. What you want to do is momentarily obstruct his vision. Then return the hand to your side. As with the corrective jerk, the movement of your hand swinging to the left and then back into place should be quick and precise.

As your left hand returns to your side, step forward and to the left on your *right* foot. Keeping your left foot in place, swivel on the balls of both feet to execute a quick about-face. You are now facing the dog. Once you have made this full turn, bring your left foot next to your right foot.

Note: You do not take that first step forward on your left foot because that is your dog's signal to move forward. For the same reason, until you are fully facing the dog, and thus blocking his forward movement, you do not lift your left leg from the floor.

Start to back away, releasing several inches of the

leash at a time. When you reach the end of the six-foot leash, stop and praise him warmly. Repeat the command "Stay." Note: In his on-leash training, your dog learned to respond to the verbal command "Stay." No additional hand motion is necessary.

Walk around the dog in a complete circle. Hold the leash with just enough slack so that you do not pull on him. Once you return to your starting position, praise him and drop the leash to the floor. With your hands at your sides, make another circle around him. Tell him what a good fellow he is. He is now ready to move on to "Sit-Stay" at a longer distance.

Step One: "Sit-Stay" at Twenty Feet

For this step you will need a long leash. Use one twenty feet or longer or tie several standard-size leashes together. Or, if you prefer, work with a clothesline.

You will also need a long working area. If you have a twenty-five-foot living room or basement, that's fine. So is the backyard or the hallway in your apartment house. If no such places are available, select a secluded, enclosed area outdoors.

Study the practice area beforehand and keep a clear picture of it in your mind. You do not want to back into some roller skates on the basement floor or the basketball pole in the school playground. Lying on your back is a tough position from which to hold your dog in "Stay."

Stand to the right of the dog and tell him to "Sit." Give him a moment to get comfortable. Then issue the command "Stay" and, quickly but smoothly, swing your left hand momentarily in front of his eyes. Step forward and to the left with your right foot, swivel on the balls of both feet, and execute a

Figures 48, 49. Long distance "Sit-Stay": With dog at end of six-foot leash attached to clothesline; with handle and clothesline.

quick about-face. Once you are facing the dog, bring your left foot back against the right one.

Start walking backward, releasing the leash as you go. Move six feet at a brisk pace. Stop, take a full circle around him, and give him praise. So far, so good. This is an old lesson for him.

Now walk back two feet more. Call out "Stay" once again and move a foot to the left. Reverse your direction and move a foot to the right. Stop and congratulate him. Do so in a soft, reassuring voice. You do not want to excite him with exuberant praise or he may decide to run up to you and lick your hand.

Continue to move from side to side, gradually extending the arc in each direction. At all times, keep enough slack in the leash so that you do not pull the dog. If at any point he attempts to move forward or turn his body toward you, stop immediately, call out "No," and deliver a correction.

It is permissible, however, for your dog to turn his head. He is more or less in the position of a spectator watching a tennis match. His head may pivot back and forth but his body must remain in place.

If he holds his stationary position, walk around him. Call out "Stay" in a soft, soothing voice at various points of your circumference. When you complete a full revolution, stop and praise him.

Holding the leash properly as you orbit your dog can be tricky. You cannot allow the leash to drag on the floor or even hang very low. The long leash or clothesline is heavy and its weight may pull the dog out of position. You should grasp it in your right hand at a point that allows enough slack between you and the dog, and hold it high (see figure 48). This takes much of the weight of the leash off your dog. The remainder of the leash may be coiled up and held in your left hand.

Practice your left and right movements and your

circles around the dog at least half a dozen times. When you are satisfied with his performance at eight feet, move back two feet more. Remember to leave enough slack in the leash so that you do not pull the dog forward. Remember, too, to hold the leash high so that it doesn't weigh the dog down.

At ten feet, stop and praise him. Move several feet to the left, then several feet to the right. Finally, walk a full circle around him. Give him praise. Repeat this procedure half a dozen times.

Midway in the session, release him from his "Sit" position. Give your dog a moment to get up and stretch. It is difficult for him to remain in the "Sit" position for longer than ten minutes at a time. Call out a cheerful "Okay." Note: In his basic training, your dog learned that one of the meanings of "Okay" is a release from his command position. I will discuss the other meaning later.

In succeeding sessions, gradually increase your distance two feet at a time until you are twenty feet away. At each distance, circle the dog half a dozen times. Your dog may start to look like a maypole, but keep it up. Repetition is the key to successful training.

If at any point along the way he turns his body or starts to walk away, call out a sharp "No" and execute a correction with the leash.

At a distance of ten feet or more, it may be a little difficult to administer an effective correction. Since you are standing in front of the dog, jerk the leash upward. Do so in a strong and rapid movement, and then relax the leash immediately.

If he moves repeatedly at, say, sixteen feet, then go back and work with him some more at fourteen feet. Work your way up to twenty feet slowly. Drill him for fifteen minutes at a time, twice a day. Be prepared to spend a full week on this step.

Step Two: Drop the Leash to the Ground

Review step one. Walk back twenty feet, stop, then circle him. Give him praise.

Drop your end of the leash to the ground. If your dog moves forward, call out "No." At this stage of his training the "No" should suffice as a correction. When he stops, praise him. Then command him to "Sit and "Stay." With your hands at your sides, start to move back slowly. At twenty-five feet, stop and tell him what a good dog he is. Then move several feet to the left. Praise him. Reverse your direction and move several feet to the right. "Good dog!" Now take a slow spin completely around him.

Figure 50. "Sit-Stay" with leash on ground.

142

If he is going to move, he will probably try it while you are circling behind him, because he cannot see you at this point. He is also aware that you are not holding onto his leash. As soon as he starts to move, call out a stern "No." Chances are he'll respond to your "No" immediately and stop. If he does, praise him and command him to "Sit" and "Stay."

Practice this exercise in fifteen-minute sessions twice a day. Be sure to break up each session at half-time to give him a chance to get up and move about. Spend at least several days on this step. Constant repetition is the cornerstone of successful training.

Figure 51. The power of "Stay."

STEP THREE: REMOVE THE LEASH AND USE THE HANDLE ONLY

Review step two. Put the dog in "Sit-Stay" and slowly back away from him to twenty feet. Then drop the leash to the ground and back away another five feet. With your hands at your sides, walk slowly around him.

If he passes this review, remove his leash and attach the *handle only* to his collar. Put him in a "Sit-Stay" position and step back three feet. Praise him. Walk a three-foot circle around him. Stop and tell him he's doing fine. If he attempts to move, reach forward, grab the handle, and execute a correction. At the same time, call out "No." Repeat this circle several times until you are satisfied that he understands, leash or no leash, that he is to remain in "Stay."

Step back three feet more, praise him, and orbit him. If he shifts his position, call out "No." At this stage, the vocal command should be enough to correct him. Walk a full circle around him. When you are satisfied with his performance at six feet, move back three feet more.

Work your way back slowly three feet at a time, until you are roughly twenty-four or twenty-five feet away from the dog. At each new distance, repeat the exercise at least a half dozen times, or until he "Stays" without moving. It should take you about a week to be able to move around him from a distance of twenty-five feet.

STEP FOUR: REMOVE THE HANDLE

Review the circle exercise with the leash handle attached to your dog's collar. He should remain in a

144

fixed position as you navigate about him at a distance of twenty-five feet.

Now, unclasp the handle. All the weight is removed from his collar and he is totally "free." He may toy with the notion of escape. The best way for you to quash such thoughts is with some psychological one-upmanship. Place his six-foot leash on the ground in front of him. Although he can't feel it, he can see it. He will reconsider any urge to take off.

Back away from him for six feet, remind him to "Stay," and describe a circle around him. Praise him. Repeat this six-foot circle several times. Then, pick up the leash, hold it in one hand, and back away another four feet. Command him to "Sit-Stay." Slap the leash against the palm of your other hand as you revolve around him. He can no longer see the leash, but he hears the occasional crack. Chances are he will stay put.

When you are satisfied with his performance as you orbit him from a distance of ten feet, increase the distance to fifteen, twenty, and twenty-five feet. With each complete circle, stop and congratulate him. Tell him how trustworthy he is. He will forget that he ever considered running away.

Now, at a distance of twenty-five feet, walk behind him, stop, and stand motionless for a full minute. Your dog will wonder where you are. If you are practicing indoors, walk into another room. Then return to your starting position and praise him.

Repeat this procedure half a dozen times. Then release him from his "Sit" position and give him a well-earned break.

Gradually, as you circle him from a distance of twenty-five feet, increase the time you "hide" from him to a full five minutes. Practice circling and disappearing in sessions of fifteen minutes, twice a day. Stay with this exercise for at least a week.

Step Five: "Sit-Stay" from a Distance

Your dog is now holding a "Sit" position from a distance of twenty-five feet. What's more, he holds it despite the absence of any leash control and despite your disappearance for several minutes at a time.

In this step, you will increase the distance between you to a point at which the dog can no longer see you at all. He will learn to respond to your vocal command only.

If you have been practicing indoors or in a small area outdoors, you will have to relocate to a more spacious area. Choose a large outdoor spot, one that is quiet and enclosed.

Review the previous step. Remove the dog's leash, put him in the "Sit" position, then back away slowly for some twenty-five feet. Stop and remind him to "Stay." Praise him. Start on a circular route around him. When you are directly behind him, stop and stand motionless for several minutes. Then return to your starting position. So far, so good.

Now take a fishline and tie one end to the dog's collar. This is not a step backward in your training. The fishline, unlike the clothesline or leash, is weightless, so the dog has the illusion of total freedom.

For effective control, keep your end of the fishline wrapped around your hand several times. Be sure to wear gloves. This will prevent the line from cutting into your skin if you have to deliver a correction.

Put your dog in a "Sit" position and walk back some thirty feet. Keep just enough slack in the line so that you are not pulling on the dog. Remind him to "Stay."

Circling the dog at this distance is impractical.

146

Substitute other methods to disappear from his view. Start a game of hide-and-seek. Walk behind a tree or a bush or a wall. After one or two minutes, step out into the open and give him a "Good boy!"

Practice disappearing and reappearing at least six times. Each time you emerge, be sure to praise him. Midway through each session, release him from his "Sit" position and let him move about. When he is performing without error at thirty feet, move back five feet more.

At some point he may become jittery about not being able to see you. If he attempts to move, be ready to correct him. Call out a "No" loud enough for him to hear across the distance between you, and execute a very strong, sharp pull on the line. Your dog won't know where the physical correction is coming from, but he will feel it and he will also hear the displeasure in your voice. When he stops moving, praise him.

Continue this procedure, moving back five feet at a time until you are roughly sixty feet from the dog.

I can hear you groaning now. You are probably growing weary of hiding behind bushes and calling out "Stay." But be patient. Remember it is only through repetition that any training of lasting value will result.

And don't try shortcuts. You cannot glance over your shoulder and, if nobody in the park is watching you, move from thirty feet to sixty feet in one go. You have to work your way out methodically, five feet at a time.

The day will finally come when, at a distance of roughly sixty feet, your dog will "Sit" for several minutes at a time. He will do so whether he sees you or not. It is then time to practice in an area with distractions.

Step Six: Practical Application

Choose some spot in the park that is thrumming
with activity. Or select an open street (but one with a
minimum of traffic). Remove your dog's leash and
attach the fishline. Tell him to "Sit" and "Stay" and
briskly walk backward some thirty feet. (Be careful
not to trip over rubbish cans or baby carriages.) Stop
and praise him.

Disappear inside a doorway or behind a tree.
Emerge and praise him. Continue moving backward,
five feet at a time. At some point he may become distracted by another dog or children playing. He may
start to move forward. Call out a sharp "No" and pull
up on the fishline. Your dog may sulk. He may howl,
"You can't trust anybody on two legs." But he will
stop and he will "Sit."

Eventually, despite distractions, he will "Sit" and
"Stay" at a distance of some sixty feet. At that time,
remove the fishline.

With the line off, you will find ample opportunities for practical application. He will "Sit-Stay" near
your bench while you go off to purchase ice cream
from the vendor in the park. He will "Sit-Stay" on a
quiet suburban street while you help your neighbor
carry some packages indoors. Note: You can now
join your neighbor in a cup of coffee, but stick to one
cup. Don't expect your dog to hold the "Sit" position
for more than ten minutes.

21

"Down - Stay"

IN HIS BASIC training, your dog learned to go "Down" at your command and to "Stay" in that position until you gave him permission to move.

He goes "Down" and "Stays" on the bathroom floor while you take a leisurely soak in the tub. He goes "Down" and "Stays" while your soufflé is rising in the oven or you are playing backgammon with your friends. Because of his good behavior he is able to remain close to household activity instead of being banished to some Siberian room.

Now you will train him to go "Down" on command, outdoors as well as in, and off his leash. He will learn to respond to your command from a long distance, and he will hold his position for as long as you wish.

Begin this command by reviewing his training on the leash. Go back to the quiet room you used for your practice sessions.

Put him in "Sit-Stay" and back away to the end of the six-foot leash. Holding the leash in your left

Figures 52, 53. Basic "Down-Stay": With dog in "Down" position, give hand and voice commands to "Stay"; repeat command with dog at end of six-foot leash.

hand, raise your right hand—fingers extended and joined, palm flat and facing the dog. As you lower your arm slowly to your side, call out the command "Down." Do not preface the command with his name. You do not want him to move forward.

The word "Down" should be drawn out so that it takes as long to say it as it does to lower your hand to your side. It should sound as if your tongue and lips got caught on the o and w. "Dooowwwn." Let your voice drop slowly in pitch.

By the time you have lowered your hand and completed the command, your dog will be in a "Down" position. Praise him. Command him to "Stay."

Walk several feet to the left, then reverse your direction and walk several feet to the right. Be certain to leave enough slack in the leash so that you do not yank the dog out of his position. It is all right for your dog to roll his eyes or pivot his head as you move horizontally in front of him, but he must not move his torso. Walk about him in a circle. Praise him and release him with an "Okay."

Drop your end of the leash to the floor. Stand six feet in front of him and raise your right arm. Call out "Down" as you slowly lower your hand to your side. Praise him and take a walk around him. If he passes this review, you are ready to begin.

Incidentally, the well-trained dog, anticipating the complete up-and-down movement of your arm, will start moving into the "Down" position the moment he sees your arm heading up. This is good. After he is trained off leash, you will have many occasions to signal him to go "Down" from a distance outdoors. You may want to stop him from hurtling headlong into a bobbing seesaw plank or a rapidly oscillating swing. The faster he stops and goes "Down," the better. For off-leash training, therefore, you should encourage and train him to respond to the "Down" command as your hand goes up.

Step One: "Down-Stay" at Twenty Feet

Get out your long leash or clothesline and go back to your basement, apartment hallway, or other spacious area. Stand eight feet in front of your dog, keeping enough slack in the leash so that you do not pull him forward.

Raise your right hand slowly into the air. At the same moment, call out the command "Down." Lower your arm, give him a "Good boy!" and tell him to "Stay." Walk a full circle around him. Hold the leash high so that its weight doesn't pull your dog's head down.

It is important that your dog realize that the hand signal—your arm going up—makes the same point

Figure 54. *"Down-Stay" with dog at end of six-foot leash attached to clothesline.*

as the verbal command. The two should become interchangeable for him. Stand eight feet in front of him. Tell him "Down" but do not move your arm. Congratulate him when he complies. Circle him.

Try it the other way. Raise your right arm but do not use the vocal command. "Atta boy!" Orbit him.

If at any point he falters and fails to go "Down," tell him "No" and execute a firm correction on the leash.

Repeat this exercise at eight feet at least half a dozen times. Use the vocal and the hand commands together, then use each one separately. Praise him with each correct performance but do not become too exuberant. Do not shout "By God, you've got it!" He may become so excited by your praise that he'll

Figure 55. *"Down-Stay" with leash on ground.*

rush up and plant a long wet thank-you kiss upon your cheek.

Note: You may find that he responds to one signal better than the other. For example, he may go "Down" immediately when he hears your vocal command but he may hesitate when you use the hand signal only. In that case, you must spend more time practicing the hand signal. Eventually he will understand that the signals are interchangeable.

When he responds to both commands with equal alacrity and understanding, advance to a distance of ten feet and repeat the procedure.

Drill your dog for fifteen minutes at a time, twice a day. When you are satisfied that he understands "Down" at ten feet, move back two feet more. At twelve feet, use the hand signal only. At fourteen feet, try the voice command alone.

Gradually work your way back, two feet at a time, until he is going "Down" and "Staying" at a distance of twenty feet.

Step Two: Drop the Leash to the Ground

Review step one. Walk back twenty feet, signal your dog to go "Down," and walk around him. Praise him.

Drop your end of the leash to the ground. With both hands hanging loosely at your sides, command him to "Stay." Step back five feet more. If he starts to move, call out a sharp "No." At this stage of training, the "No" should suffice as a correction.

With the leash on the floor and your hands at your sides, move several feet to the left. Then reverse your direction and move several feet to the right. Finally, walk completely around him.

Stay with this exercise for several days.

Step Three: Remove the Leash and Use the Handle Only

Put the long leash or clothesline on your dog. Review step two. Walk back twenty feet, releasing the leash as you go. Raise your right arm and call out "Down." Praise him. Drop your end of the leash to the ground, back away five feet more, and walk slowly around him. "Good dog!"

If he passes this review, remove his leash and attach the *handle only* to his collar. Stand directly in front of him, raise your right arm, and call out "Down."

With the weight of the leash removed, he may hesitate before assuming the "Down" position. Step forward, grab the handle, and administer a quick, firm correction. At the same time, call out a stern "No!" Jerking the handle requires special caution. Do not jerk it forward or your dog may come running toward you. Jerk it downward. When he assumes the "Down" position, praise him. Command him to "Stay" and walk a full circle around him.

Alternate your commands. Use the vocal command alone and then the hand signal only. After each command, walk completely around him.

Repeat this drill until he goes "Down" without correction, in response to either or both of your commands, at least half a dozen times.

Walk back three feet, and repeat the procedure.

If he performs properly with the hand signal but falters when you employ the voice command, then give more attention to the latter. Work your way out slowly, three feet at a time, until you are roughly twenty-four or twenty-five feet from your dog. At each new distance, repeat the exercise at least half a dozen times. Practice for fifteen minutes, twice a day.

155

Figure 56. "Down-Stay" with handle only.

Figure 57. "Down-Stay" with no restrictions on dog.

Step Four: "Down" While at Play

Now that he understands "Down" within the context of a training session, it is time to introduce the command in an informal situation.

Go back to your practice area. Clip the leash handle onto his collar.

Review his "formal" training at three feet. Stand in front of him, raise your right hand, and call out "Down." Praise him.

Relax and have some fun. Walk up to him and engage him in a playful wrestling match. Then, while his tail is wagging and his spirits are high, stand straight, raise your right hand, and call out "Down."

He may protest that it's too early to end the game. If he fails to respond, reach for the handle and execute a quick, firm correction. Remember to yank the handle downward.

If he has absorbed all his training thus far, chances are he'll slip into the "Down" position immediately. Congratulate him. Go back to the formal "Down." Stand three feet in front of him and use the vocal command only. Praise him as he goes "Down."

Switch to play. Run about your practice area and encourage him to chase you. After several minutes, or before you are reduced to a state of exhaustion, stop and raise your right hand. Do not speak. He should skid to a stop and go "Down." Praise him.

Alternate the formal "Down" with the command while he is absorbed in play. Use both the hand and voice signals together, and then use each signal alone. He is gradually learning that a signal from you—whether it is your voice or your hand—takes precedence over fun and games.

STEP FIVE: NO LEASH CONTROL

Go back and review step three. Attach the handle to the dog's collar, back away twenty-five feet, and run through the "Down" command. Use both the hand and voice signals together, and then use each signal alone. When he responds without error, unclasp the handle. All physical control is removed.

While the innocent look on his face implies that he would never break his training, it is best at this point to arm yourself with some psychological control. Place his six-foot leash on the ground in front of him. He cannot feel it but he can see it and smell it. He will remain in place.

Walk back five feet, raise your right arm, and tell him "Down." Give him praise. Walk a full circle around him. Remember, he is allowed to move his eyes and his head, but his body must remain stationary.

Pick up the leash, hold it in your hand, and walk back another five feet. Give him the "Down" command. Slap the leash against the palm of your other hand as you circle him. Your dog no longer sees the leash but he hears the occasional crack. Chances are he will stay put.

Increase the distance between you and your dog five feet at a time. At each step along the way, practice the command by using the hand and voice signals together, then each one separately. As you complete your circle at each five-foot interval, give him praise.

At a distance of twenty-five feet, walk behind him and stand, hidden from his view, for half a minute. If you are practicing indoors, walk into another room. When you return to your starting position, stop and praise him.

Continue to circle him, gradually increasing the

time you remain "hidden" until he is alone for several minutes at a time.

If curiosity gets the better of him and he attempts to follow you, call out "No!" At this stage of his training the verbal correction should be all that is necessary. Then praise him and repeat the command "Down."

Continue to circle him from a distance of twenty-five feet and to "disappear" behind him for several minutes at a time. Practice a full fifteen minutes, twice a day. Stay with this exercise for at least a week.

STEP SIX: "DOWN-STAY" FROM A DISTANCE

Your dog is now responding to your command from a distance of twenty-five feet. He is remaining in "Down-Stay" despite the absence of any leash control and despite your disappearance for several minutes at a time.

In this step you will increase the distance to some fifty or sixty feet. He will respond to your vocal command even if he cannot see you, or he will react to your hand signal if he sees but cannot hear you.

It will be necessary to move to more spacious ground. Choose a large outdoor area but one that is quiet and enclosed.

Review the previous step. Remove the dog's leash and back away slowly for twenty-five feet. Raise your right hand and call out "Down." Praise him. Start a walk around him and, when you have completed a semicircle, stop and stand motionless for several minutes. Return to your starting position and give him praise.

Now tie one end of your fishline to the dog's collar. Let me remind you again that this is *not* a step backward. The fishline, unlike the leash or clothesline, is weightless. Your dog continues to feel totally free.

Back away about thirty feet from your dog. Leave enough slack in the line so that you are not pulling on the dog's collar. For better control, wrap the fishline around your hand several times. And remember to wear gloves.

Raise your right arm and call out "Down." Praise him.

At this distance, circling the dog becomes impractical. Substitute other methods to disappear from his view. Hide behind a tree or the corner of a building. Remain out of sight for several minutes at a time. But at all times, keep your eye on your dog. If he turns his body or moves forward, be ready to correct him. Call out a resounding "No" loud enough for him to hear across the distance between you and execute a very strong, sharp pull on the line.

Your dog won't know where the physical correction comes from, but he will feel it. He won't know where your voice comes from, but he will hear it. When he stops, step into the open and praise him. Then raise your arm and call out "Down."

Practice disappearing and reappearing at this distance of thirty feet at least half a dozen times. If he holds the "Down" position without error, move back five feet more.

Several minutes before the session is over, remove the fishline. It is time to practice "Down" under informal circumstances. Start to jog around the area and encourage him to join you. Stop suddenly, raise your right arm, and call out "Down."

If he stands and sulks because the fun is over, call out a sharp "No." At this stage of his training, the vocal correction should be adequate. Signal him once again to go "Down." Praise him warmly.

Start each new session by attaching the fishline. Work your way back five feet at a time. At each new position, practice the exercise at least half a dozen times. Use both hand and voice signals together, then use each one alone.

Toward the end of each session, remove the fishline and spend several minutes in free play. Practice the informal "Down."

It may take several weeks, but eventually your dog will follow your command to go "Down" from a distance of some sixty feet. In addition, he will maintain the "Down" position when you disappear from view, until you reappear and release him. You will then be ready for the final step.

STEP SEVEN: PRACTICAL APPLICATION

Choose an area of the park that is populated with people and other dogs. Or select an open street (but one with a minimum of traffic).

Remove his leash and tie one end of the fishline to his collar. Be sure to wear your gloves. Tell him to "Stay," then turn and walk away. Keep enough slack in the line so that you do not pull on the dog.

As you increase the distance between you, your palms may turn moist and your mouth may go dry. Your dog is a long way off, in an area with many temptations. Will he break his "Stay" position to follow some irresistible temptation? Relax. There is no need to worry. Instead, keep a tight hold on your fishline.

At a distance of about thirty feet, turn to him, raise your right arm, and call out "Down." Praise him in soft, soothing tones. Disappear inside a doorway or behind a tree. Emerge and praise him. Practice the command using the voice and hand signals together, then each one separately.

162

At some point, his attention may wander. He may become engrossed in watching a game of hopscotch or fascinated by the animated conversation of some strangers nearby. Expect this and be prepared for it. If he doesn't heed your command, pull up sharply on the fishline and shout out "No!" Raise your right arm and tell him "Down." Praise him.

Repeat this exercise until he performs correctly at least half a dozen times in a row. Practice for fifteen minutes at a time, twice a day.

When you are satisfied with his performance at thirty feet, move back ten feet more. Repeat the procedure at forty, fifty, and sixty feet.

The day will finally arrive when, from a distance of roughly sixty feet, in an area alive with distractions, he will heed your command to go "Down." He will respond with equal alacrity whether he sees your hand go up or hears your vocal command. He will remain in that position, whether or not he is able to see you, until you give him permission to move. On that day, you may reel in your fishline and consider his "Down" training complete.

22

"Come When Called"

You our dog has now learned to "Heel" without a leash, to "Sit" off leash while you wander out of sight, to heed your command from afar to go "Down." Now comes the most important command in off-leash training: "Come When Called."

It is also the most difficult command to teach. It will require all the patience you can muster, all the energy you have. It will also require all the time you can spare.

Keep in mind that the effort will be worth it. The dog who knows this command will come to you immediately, regardless of the distance between you, regardless of his involvement in other activities, regardless of his absorption in other people or objects nearby. And when he reaches you, he will drop into a "Sit" position in front of you.

Having the dog come when you call him is more than a matter of convenience. It could very well save his life.

In teaching this command, praise is of the utmost

importance. You may call your dog to you for a variety of reasons, but when he arrives at your feet your response must always be the same: total, exuberant praise.

Remember, you are competing for his attention with all the temptations in the area. He must feel that answering your call is more exciting than staying with or plunging into the hubbub and bustle going on about him. He must believe that the welcome that awaits him is far more exhilarating than observing and listening to the passing parade.

Praise is what motivates him to drop what he is doing and run to your side. Praise is his incentive to stop his explorations and answer your call. Make it worth his while. Give him hearty, unstinting praise.

There will be times when he misbehaves and it will be necessary to correct him. *Go to him to do it!* If you spy him pawing at your neighbor's flower bed, go to him and tell him "No." Never call him to you to correct or scold him. He will very quickly lose all incentive to answer your call.

Say you spot him slinking around a hot-dog stand. Call him to you, then praise him for pulling himself away from such tantalizing smells. If you see him snooping near two lovers in the grass, call him to you. Praise him for giving up his ringside seat.

Remember, whenever he comes to you, praise him. If he needs correction, go to him.

In this command, we use three words: "Okay, [Name], come."

The word "Okay" is a happy one for your dog. In training, it has two uses. First, it is a release from his last command position. Tell him "Okay" and he'll scramble to his feet from his "Sit-Stay" or "Down-Stay" posture. The second use of the word "Okay" is to set the mood of the next command. It is always delivered in a light and cheerful tone. It conveys to your dog that something warm and wonderful is in store for him. It alerts him to pay attention. It is in this sense that "Okay" is employed in "Come When Called."

The second word—his name—is used in all forward-action commands. The sound of his name is a signal to the dog to get ready to move forward.

The third word, "Come," tells him what he must do. He must run to you, stop in front of you, and automatically sit.

The importance of sitting automatically will become apparent when your dog starts coming to you from afar. If he isn't accustomed to sitting in front of you, he might, like an Olympic runner, dash past the finish line and wind up somewhere behind you.

Start by reviewing "Come When Called" on leash. Put him in a "Sit-Stay" position and back away to the end of the six-foot leash. Leave just enough slack in the leash so you do not pull on him. Let's say your dog's name is Bernie. Give him the command "Okay, Bernie, come."

At the same time, use your hand signal. Lift your right arm up to shoulder level and then swing it across your chest. The gesture is the same you use when you beckon someone to you.

When he trots up to you and sits, give him warm, exuberant praise. You are now ready to begin.

Step One: "Come When Called"
at Twenty Feet

Get out your long leash or clothesline and go back to your basement, backyard, or apartment hallway. Put your dog in "Sit-Stay." Slowly back away, releasing the leash as you go. Leave enough slack in the leash so you do not pull the dog forward. When

Figures 58, 59. Positions for "Come When Called": with six-foot leash; with twenty-foot clothesline.

you are standing eight feet in front of him, stop and praise him.

Give him the command "Okay, Bernie, come." Call it out cheerfully. At the same moment you issue the voice command, use the hand signal. Raise your right arm in front of you and, in a beckoning gesture, swing it across your chest. If he responds immediately, if he runs up and sits directly in front of you, praise him warmly.

His immediate response is extremely important. Many times, it can prevent a dogfight. It can also save his life. Do not allow him to dawdle. Do not allow him to finish his daydream before answering your call.

If he hesitates before running to you, be ready to correct him. Jerk the leash and call out a stern "No." Then start over. Gesture with your right arm and put on a happy face as you call out once again "Okay, Bernie, come." Tell him he's a great dog!

It is important that your dog associate your hand signal—your arm sweeping across your chest—with your verbal command. The two should become interchangeable for him. Stand eight feet in front of him and call out "Okay, Bernie, come," but do not move your arm. When he heeds your call by itself, give him a "Good boy!"

Try it the other way. Swing your arm across your chest but do not use the vocal command. "Smart fella!"

Stay with this exercise for several days, or until your dog performs without error at least half a dozen times in a row. Use both the verbal and hand signals together, then use each one alone.

Work your way back two feet at a time until you are commanding him to "Come" from a distance of twenty feet.

Holding the leash properly at this distance requires some dexterity. You do not want the dog to trip over the leash as he hurries to obey your command. Swing your arm outward to get the leash out of his way.

Work with him for fifteen minutes at a time and hold two sessions a day. Since your dog will be spending much of this time in the "Sit" position, be sure to give him a break midway in each practice session.

Step Two: Remove the Leash and Use the Handle and the Fishline

Go back to your practice area and review step one. Tie the long leash onto your dog's collar and put him into the "Sit" position. Tell him to "Stay." Back away twenty feet, beckon him with your right hand, and call out "Okay, Bernie, come." Praise him.

Now remove the leash and attach just the handle to the collar. Tie the fishline onto the handle. Note: The fishline gives you the same control you had in step one. Because it is weightless, however, the dog feels only the leash handle. For your dog, this is one step closer to freedom. Slip on a pair of gloves.

Put your dog in a "Sit-Stay" position and stand five feet in front of him. Call out "Okay, Bernie, come." At the same moment, beckon him with your arm. If he runs up to you immediately and sits directly in front of you, tell him how wonderful he is.

If, however, he sits watching the leaves rustle in the wind, be ready to correct him. Pull sharply on the fishline and tell him "No." Repeat your command. Praise him when he performs.

Use the verbal and hand signals together, then drill him using each signal alone.

Stay with this exercise at a distance of five feet until he performs without error at least half a dozen times in a row. Then step back five feet more. Repeat the exercise at ten, fifteen, twenty, and twenty-five feet.

As the distance between you lengthens, his performance may become sloppy. For example, at fifteen feet he may start to run ahead before you call to him.

If that occurs, you will have to review the "Sit-Stays." Put him in a "Sit-Stay" position, walk back *ten feet only*, face him and stand perfectly still. Say nothing. If he starts to move forward, give him a physical correction and tell him "No." Repeat the command "Stay" and walk a full circle around him.

Repeat this drill half a dozen times. Then try the "Come When Called" command. Put him in "Sit-Stay," walk back ten feet, face him, and call him to "Come." When he runs to you, praise him.

Alternate circling him as he "Sit-Stays" at ten feet with giving him the "Come When Called" command. Your dog may wish you'd make up your mind, but he is learning one thing: He must not anticipate your commands.

When you are satisfied with his performance at ten feet, move back once again to fifteen. Continue this exercise until he is coming to you, without error, from a distance of roughly twenty-five feet.

It is good to praise him while he is in the act of running to you. This will help keep his mind on what he started out to do. Call out "Good boy!" "Atta boy!" "Hooray for the Mets!" It doesn't matter what you say. What is important is that you pack lots of enthusiasm into your voice.

Stay with this exercise for about a week. Practice in fifteen-minute sessions, twice a day.

STEP THREE: FREE PLAY

Return to your practice area. Remove the leash and attach the handle to his collar. Tie the fishing line to the handle.

Review step two. Put him in a "Sit-Stay" position and walk back twenty-five feet. Call out "Okay, Bernie, come," and beckon him with your right arm. Praise him.

Repeat this exercise using the vocal command only. Try it a third time with the hand signal only.

Now release him with an "Okay" and let him wander about. Keep some twenty-five feet away from him and while he is absorbed in sniffing the concrete or the carpet on the floor, give him the command, "Okay, Bernie, come." Beckon him with your arm.

If he runs to you immediately and sits at your feet, give him exuberant praise. He may, however, toss you a disdainful look and go on with his examinations.

Pull sharply on the line and tell him "No." Repeat the "Come When Called" command once again. Praise him when he complies. Stay with this exercise until he is responding to your call under "informal" circumstances—while his attention is elsewhere—at least a half dozen times in a row.

Now remove the fishing line. Command him to "Sit-Stay," then turn and run quickly ahead. When you are roughly twenty-five feet away, turn back in his direction and call him to "Come." This is his idea of fun! He'll probably grin like a Halloween pumpkin, sprint after you, and skid to a stop at your feet.

Try the informal command once again. Call to him while his attention is elsewhere. If he fails to respond immediately, or if he stops to scratch his ear along the way, it will be necessary to go back a half step and tie the fishline to the handle.

Be prepared to take such an occasional step backward. Do not be discouraged if your dog does not progress smoothly from one phase to the next, or if he doesn't master every exercise as quickly as the one before. Go back and spend a day or two in review.

Your attitude is extremely important. Do not let any disappointment show. Do not tell him he is an underachiever, and that he'll never make it. Nor should you wallow in guilt and wonder where you went wrong.

Be patient, be optimistic, be cheerful. Keep in mind that it is repetition that reinforces his understanding and leads to permanent results.

Work at this exercise for fifteen minutes at a time, twice a day. When he answers your call from a distance of twenty-five feet, without any line control and while absorbed in "free play," move on to the next step.

STEP FOUR: "COME WHEN CALLED" FROM A DISTANCE

In this step you will practice the command at distances up to fifty or sixty feet. It will be necessary to relocate to a larger training area. Choose a large outdoor area, one that is quiet and enclosed.

Review step three. Attach the leash handle to your dog's collar and tie one end of the fishline to the handle. Put him in "Sit-Stay," walk away twenty-five feet, and give him the "Come When Called" command. Praise him.

Remove the handle and tie just the fishline to the collar. With the handle off, your dog feels absolutely free. That's why you are using the fishline. The line is so light that your dog is unaware of it, but it still leaves you with complete physical control. Don't forget your gloves.

Put him in a "Sit-Stay" position and back away about twenty-five feet. Leave enough slack in the line so you do not pull the dog forward. Call out "Okay, Bernie, come," and beckon him with your right hand. If he comes, quickly and without hesitation, and drops to a "Sit" position in front of you, give him lots of praise.

If he hesitates, pull sharply on the line and call out a stern "No." Your dog may be astonished and wonder where the correction is coming from, but it is something he will not easily forget.

Try the "Come When Called" command again. Be ready to give him enthusiastic praise.

Practice the command with the hand signal only, then use the verbal signal only. Perform this exercise at twenty-five feet until he responds flawlessly at least half a dozen times in a row.

Proceed to the "informal" command. Release him with an "Okay," stay twenty-five feet away until he relaxes and turns his attention elsewhere, then call out "Okay, Bernie, come." Praise him warmly. "What a good boy!""What a smart boy!" If his tail wags furiously as he sits before you, if it whips the ground and scatters pebbles about, you are giving him adequate praise.

Gradually work your way back five feet at a time, until you are calling him to come from a distance of some fifty or sixty feet. Alternate calling him while he is in a "Sit-Stay" position and while he is moving freely about.

Remember to cheer him on as he runs the long distance toward you. This will help keep his mind on what he started out to do.

There is still the possibility, however, that somewhere along the way he may become distracted and take off suddenly in another direction. Hang on to your fishline. When he reaches the end of the line, pull sharply on it and call out a loud "No."

On the other hand, he may be so eager to reach you that he barrels toward you with the speed of a race-horse coming down the homestretch.

Do not panic. Do not cringe or turn and run the other way.

When he is some ten feet in front of you and it looks as if he has no intention of stopping, call out "Stay." Draw the word out: "Sta-a-a-y." This will slow him down and get him to stop in front of you in time. Note: He may react to your "Stay" by slowing to a crawl. In that case, call out once again "Okay, Bernie, come."

You may have to spend several weeks on this exercise, until he performs it without error while you still maintain physical control. Do not become impatient and overlook little errors or disregard certain imperfections in his response. If he performs improperly while the fishline is on, he will perform improperly with the fishline off. His mistakes will not disappear by themselves. Work with him, correct him, praise him. Stay with this exercise until he responds without error several days in a row. Work at it in fifteen-minute sessions, twice a day.

Step Five: No Physical Control

Return to your practice area and bring the throw chain with you. Remove the leash. You will now practice the command without any physical controls.

Figures 60, 61, 62. "Come When Called" with no physical control.

174

Put your dog in the "Sit-Stay" position and back away some twenty-five feet. Call out "Okay, Bernie, come," and beckon him with your hand. If he starts up immediately, runs to you in a straight line, and drops promptly to a "Sit" position in front of you, give him lots of praise.

Try the exercise with the verbal and hand signals separately. Then work at the informal command. Release him from his "Sit" position with a cheerful "Okay" and proceed to walk away. At a distance of roughly twenty-five feet, stop and wait. Let him wander about and amuse himself. Then, while his attention is diverted, call out the command "Okay, Bernie, come," and beckon him with your hand.

If he fails to respond, toss the throw chain in front of him and call out a stern "No," timing it to coincide with the chain hitting the ground. Repeat the command. When he runs and sits in front of you, give him enthusiastic praise.

Your dog may decide not to answer your call, or he may suddenly take off in another direction. Do not give in to the temptation to run after him. Turn his misbehavior into a game. Run the other way. Your dog loves a good game of tag and will probably reverse his direction and chase after you. Make certain you turn toward him as he catches up to you. Then, when he sits at your feet, tell him how well behaved he is for coming when you called.

I know what you're thinking. Maybe you can fool someone else's dog with a game like that, but not mine.

Okay, with some dogs you have to try a little harder. Let's say he looks at you with disdain while you run off in the other direction. Keep running and circling, patting your thigh and calling out, "Okay, Bernie, come." Use a cheerful, enticing tone. The sun may start to set in the sky and the lights flicker on in apartments and houses all over town. Continue to run away from him and call to him. Keep your tone cheerful and inviting.

Sooner or later, he will come. When he does, turn and face him. As he skids to a stop in front of you, do not give in to your impulse to strangle him. Instead, unclench your fists, ungrit your teeth and . . . smile! Praise him! "What a good boy you are!" "What a smart boy!"

Keep in mind that a dog's failure to obey is often the result of too little praise. You may think you are overdoing it, you may feel you have reached a saturation point, but don't stop. With a dog, flattery will get you everywhere.

Work your way back five feet at a time. Alternate giving the command formally—when he is in the "Sit-Stay" position—and informally—when he is at ease. Spend a full fifteen minutes at it and come back to your practice area twice a day.

When he is coming to you repeatedly without error from a distance of fifty feet, move to the next step.

STEP SIX: PRACTICAL APPLICATION

It is time for practical application. Walk to a busy area in the park. Or select an open street (but one with a minimum of traffic).

Remove your dog's leash and tie the fishline to his collar. Be sure to wear gloves.

Put your dog in a "Sit-Stay" position and back away ten feet. Leave enough slack in the line so you do not pull your dog forward. Call out "Okay, Bernie, come," and beckon him with your arm. Praise him warmly when he complies.

Release him from the "Sit" position and walk ten

feet away. Let him roam about the area and then, when he is absorbed, say, in watching a mother rock her baby's carriage, call him to you. Praise him effusively.

Back away ten feet at a time. Practice the command in a formal setup—while he is in the "Sit" position—then try it informally—while he is moving freely about.

If at any point he fails to respond, call out "No" and give him a physical correction with the line.

If he is distracted easily, then it will be necessary to go back to your secluded area and pick up his training in private. Do not be discouraged. In the open area, you are competing with a myriad of sights and sounds and smells. Spend several days in quiet practice. Then bring him out to your busy area once again.

Practice the command for fifteen minutes at a time and hold two sessions a day. Spend at least a week in this busy area, with the line attached to your dog's collar. Work your way up gradually to a distance of fifty or sixty feet.

When he responds without error from this distance at least half a dozen times in a row, he is ready for the same exercise without the fishline between you. Repeat it until you feel sure of his responsiveness in a variety of situations.

23

"Go to Heel"

OFTEN YOU WILL want to move your dog from "Come When Called" to "Heel" at your side. Shifting him from the "Sit" position in front of you to a standing position at your left side is the purpose of the "Go to Heel" command.

"Go to Heel" completes the "Come When Called" command and is the finishing touch to off-leash training.

STEP ONE: "GO TO HEEL" WITH THE LEASH ON

Choose a quiet room in your house and attach your dog's collar and six-foot leash. Stand in front of him with your arms at your sides. Give him the command "Sit." Praise him. Reach forward with your left hand and grasp the leash roughly eighteen inches from the collar. Pull it toward you. At the same moment, step back on your left foot and call out the command "Heel." This movement will bring your dog to his feet and heading toward your left side (see figure

64). Do not, in this case, use his name. Although you want your dog to shift his position, this is not a forward-action command.

Continue to pull gently on the leash until the dog is at your left side. Then, still exerting pressure on the leash, pull it slightly to the right and forward. Your hand movement will guide your dog into an about-face on your left side so that he winds up standing alongside you in the classic "Heel" position. Complete the maneuver by bringing your left foot forward to meet your right foot.

He will no doubt be clumsy the first half a dozen times. He will lurch forward and zigzag his way uncertainly around the turn. And more than likely he will arrive in the "Heel" position leaning against you like a drunk resting against a lamppost for support. No matter. He is learning what is expected of him. Keep showering him with praise. Remember that he is being conditioned to respond to three signals. He hears your vocal command "Heel." He sees your left arm moving backward. And he sees you step back on your left foot.

As you continue to practice this exercise, keep aiming for a more polished performance. You want him to rise immediately at your command, walk past your left side in a straight line, and execute a quick left about-face. You want him to complete the exercise standing in the "Heel" position with his forepaws aligned with your legs.

If, after several sessions, he comes into the "Heel" position a foot or two ahead of you, or if he halts a foot or two behind you, or if he comes to a stop several feet wide of your left side, jerk the leash and tell him "No." In each instance, follow the correction by patting your thigh to encourage him into place. If he arrives in the "Heel" position by brushing up against you, use your knee to guide him into position. After each correction, praise him.

Work with him until he is performing correctly. Practice this exercise for fifteen minutes, twice a day.

Step Two: Remove the Leash and Use the Handle Only

Go back to your practice area. Remove your dog's leash and attach just the handle to his collar. Put him in a "Sit-Stay" position. Stand directly in front of him with your arms hanging at your sides. Reach forward with your left hand, grasp the handle, and pull it toward you. At the same moment, move one step back on your left foot, and call out the command "Heel." Guide him into an about-face on your left side. When he arrives in the "Heel" position at your left side, praise him.

Guiding him with the handle takes more dexterity than working with the leash. But your dog is familiar with what is expected of him and will probably offer little resistance as you pull him toward you, turn him about, and lead him into the "Heel" position.

If he cannot seem to get the hang of it, if he pirouettes or does figure eights along the way, then it will be necessary to go back to step one and give him additional training on the leash. Then, when he is again doing it right, try it with the handle once more.

Work with him for fifteen minutes twice a day. Give him time to associate the verbal command "Heel" with your left hand and foot going backward. Stay with this step until he is performing with accuracy and speed.

Step Three: No Leash Control

Take your dog for his elimination walk, then return to your practice area. Remove the leash from his collar.

181

Figures 63, 64, 65, 66, 67, 68.
"Go to Heel": Starting "Sit"
position with dog facing
you on leash; step back
with left foot and pull back
while giving verbal com-
mand to "Heel"; with dog at
your side, pull inward and
foreward to swing dog
around . . .

. . . Dog has completed turn; dog sits, still under pulling pressure; relax pressure.

Put him in a "Sit-Stay" position in front of you. Call out the command "Heel." At the same moment, take one step backward on your left foot and swing your left arm back. Keep your arm straight, your fingers together and extended downward.

Your dog is now conditioned to move when he hears your command and sees your left arm and leg move backward. He will no doubt rise and step into the "Heel" position at your side. Tell him he is marvelous.

Repeat this exercise, using all three signals, half a dozen times in a row. When you are satisfied with his performance, *eliminate the foot signal.* Note: When you were maneuvering him into the "Heel" position with leash and handle, you had to step back on your left leg to maintain balance. Now that he is going into the "Heel" position by himself, there is no need to shift your weight. Call out "Heel" and swing your left arm back. Do not move your foot.

Your dog is much too tactful to remind you that you forgot to move your foot. Instead, he will take notice of your voice command and your arm signal and will quickly "Go to Heel." Give him exuberant praise.

Drill him until he responds to the vocal and hand signals immediately and without error at least half a dozen times in a row.

STEP FOUR: "GO TO HEEL"
FOLLOWS THE "COME WHEN CALLED" COMMAND

In this step, you will combine "Come When Called" with "Go to Heel." You will have to move to more spacious grounds. Choose an outdoor area that is quiet and enclosed. Remove your dog's leash. Put him in a "Sit-Stay" position and move ten feet away from him. Let's say his name is Norman. Call out "Okay, Norman, come." When he runs up to you and sits before you, give him praise. Wait a moment, then move your left arm back and tell him to "Heel." If he springs up and goes immediately into the "Heel" position, let him know how delighted you are.

Practice the "Come When Called" command together with "Go to Heel" at least half a dozen times at this distance. When you are satisfied with his performance, move back ten feet more. Continue the exercise until he is coming to you and then going into the "Heel" position from a distance of fifty or sixty feet.

The alert dog may come to the conclusion that, once you issue the "Come When Called" command, you follow it up with the "Go to Heel." Since he is aware that the shortest distance between two points is a straight line, he may decide to bypass the "Sit" position and run directly to your left side.

He must not fuse the two commands into one. Impress on him that they are separate and distinct instructions, and that one doesn't necessarily follow the other.

You do this by breaking up the pattern of your commands. Follow the "Come When Called" with an exercise in "Sit-Stays." Call him to you and, when he sits at your feet, tell him to "Stay." Walk a full circle about him. Praise him and release him with an "Okay."

Try the "Come When Called" command again. When he sits before you, move your left arm back and tell him to "Heel."

By alternating your commands, you keep him from anticipating what comes next. He will have to sit and watch and wait. He will have to follow one command at a time.

Step Five: Practical Application

It is time for the grand finale: a tossed salad of all the commands.

Walk with your dog to a busy section in the park. Or choose an open street (but one that has a minimum of traffic). Remove your dog's leash and allow him to roam about the area. Walk some fifty feet away from him. Raise your right arm and call out "Down." Praise him in soft soothing tones. After several minutes, tell him "Okay, Norman, come." When he runs to you and sits before you, walk a full circle about him. Stop, swing your left arm backward, and say "Heel." Once he is standing at your left side, call out "Norman, heel." Nudge him on the ear and move forward on your left foot. Head back to your house.

When you arrive home. release him with an "Okay." Tell him he's passed the course. Tell him how proud you are. Then pull out two glasses and set the champagne in a bucket of ice.

V

Dog Breeds and Their Training

AFGHAN HOUND

The Afghan combines a delicate, long-limbed beauty with an elegant, refined manner. His haughty carriage seems to suggest that he belongs to a VIP.

He is a one-person dog. He is devoted to his master but is not particularly fond of children. Supersensitive and skittish, he shies away from their rough-house play.

This aristocratic animal creates a variety of obedience problems in the city. He learns his housebreaking routine slowly. If he is alone in an apartment, he is apt to wander through the rooms, chewing all the furniture in his path.

Country living presents its own problems. Out in the yard, he busies himself digging holes in the ground. He hurls himself repeatedly against the fence.

Start his obedience training as soon as he arrives in your home. Be patient. He learns slowly.

His long silky hair requires daily grooming. The Afghan fares best with an owner who enjoys fussing with his pet, who takes pride in his beauty and has time to devote to him.

Off-Leash Training

The Afghan is a difficult dog to train off leash. He is stubborn, inattentive to his lessons, and has no strong desire to please. Be patient and use a firm hand.

Once he learns the commands, you cannot count on him to honor his training. At the sight of a distant rabbit, he will take off in a great burst of speed. In both the city and the country, restrict his freedom to a completely enclosed area in a playground or park.

189

AIREDALE TERRIER

The Airedale is the largest of the Terriers and, in terms of temperament, the easiest to live with. Alert and even tempered, he adapts well to either a city or a country environment.

An energetic fellow, he loves to jump on furniture and dig in the yard. If he lives in the country and spends his days outdoors, he will scoop out large quantities of soil from your yard.

Start his obedience training early and use a firm hand. He is extremely responsive and will quickly learn the code of behavior he must follow in your home. His housebreaking proceeds smoothly.

Because he is highly dependable and responsive to training, he is frequently used as a guide dog for the blind.

He takes great pride in guarding his property and the members of his family. He makes an exuberant playmate for the children and a devoted companion to adults.

His short, wiry coat needs professional trimming every six to eight weeks.

Off-Leash Training

The Airedale Terrier is a fine candidate for training. He has the stubborn streak of the Terrier and will, at first, try to divert you from his lessons. Be firm with him. Once he buckles down to work, he learns quickly. He performs the commands with accuracy and speed.

AKITA

This little-known canine is the newest recognized member of the Working breeds. He is large and sturdy and possesses an incredible amount of en-

190

ergy, and is therefore happier in the country, where he is able to spend many hours of the day outdoors. Keep him in an enclosed backyard.

If you live in the city, plan a vigorous physical workout for him in the morning and again at night. It will be helpful if someone can take him out in the middle of the day for an additional exercise period.

Do not confine him to a small area in your house. He will attempt to break out of it. Otherwise, his household behavior is impeccable. Highly intelligent, he responds readily to housebreaking and quickly learns the standards of behavior he must follow in the house.

Off-Leash Training

The Akita is a difficult candidate for off-leash training. Although he learns the commands easily, you cannot count on him to obey you once he is trained. He tends to be stubborn and hardheaded and he likes to have his own way. The male of this breed is frequently a dog fighter.

Limit his freedom off leash to completely enclosed areas. If your Akita proves to be a dog fighter and there are other male dogs around, do not remove his leash at all when outdoors.

ALASKAN MALAMUTE

This rugged sled dog is best suited to country living. He adapts to any climate and is capable of withstanding the rigors of subzero weather. He adores family life and relishes the rough and tumble of children's games.

What he cannot cope with is confinement indoors. If he is left alone in an apartment, he is apt to tear through it on a chewing and howling rampage.

191

If you must be out of your apartment all day, plan a vigorous exercise period for him before you leave in the morning and another when you arrive home at night. Arrange for someone to take him out for an additional workout in the middle of the day.

The key to living successfully with him in the city is early obedience training. Start working with him the moment he arrives in your home. After five or six months of age, he tends to become set in his ways and training is much more difficult.

He will take advantage of a timid master. On the other hand, strong-arm tactics and constant scolding make him aggressive. What gets him to sit up and take notice, what he responds to and respects, is firm and consistent control.

Off-Leash Training

The Alaskan Malamute is a reluctant candidate for off-leash training. He doesn't work to please you; he works because he recognizes that he has no choice. Do not be unrealistic in your expectations. He learns slowly. It takes him time to understand the "Heel" and "Come When Called." Be patient with him and exercise a firm hand.

AUSTRALIAN TERRIER

This sturdy little fellow is a bundle of perpetual motion. While his nonstop activity makes him a difficult companion for the elderly, he is wonderful for a large family. He adores children. The rougher they play, the better he likes it.

He makes a fine pet either in a city or in the country. Although he is constantly on the move, he is not a noisy dog. His housebreaking proceeds smoothly and he learns quickly what he may and may not do in your house.

If you live in the city and leave him alone indoors all day, plan several workouts. Take him out for a vigorous exercise period in the morning before you leave, and again when you arrive home at night. The more exercise he receives, the better.

Off-Leash Training

You will find it easy to train the Australian Terrier off leash. His movements are agile and swift and he learns quickly. When you call him to come, he will beat a path to your feet.

He has, however, a great need to keep moving. To hold his attention you must be firm in your approach. If he senses hesitation or weakness on your part, he may take advantage of it. He may stroll off and amuse himself elsewhere.

The same situation holds true once he is trained. At any time, the sound of some action around the corner may entice him to run away. This is especially true of the male. Limit his freedom off leash to areas that are completely enclosed. Playgrounds and fenced parks are fine.

BASENJI

The Basenji has the distinction of being a barkless dog. He does, however, have his own set of vocal responses. He growls at strangers, whines when he is lonely, and makes a chortling sound to show his pleasure.

The Basenji is also known for the "human" look on his face. The wrinkles on his forehead frequently give him a puzzled expression as if he were pondering the eccentricities of his master's behavior.

193

He is not an affectionate dog but he does attach himself with extreme loyalty to one person. For this reason, he makes a good city pet for someone living alone.

If you are a working person, however, be prepared to face certain obedience problems. The Basenji gets into mischief when he is left alone. He jumps on the furniture and chews on the drapes. On the other hand, he presents no difficulty in housebreaking.

Because of his aloof personality, he does not make a good country dog. He is reserved with large families and he definitely shies away from children and their games.

Off-Leash Training

The Basenji is a stubborn and strong-willed little fellow and will fight you at every step of his training. Be patient and exercise a firm hand. If he understands that you are the boss, he will make an effort to pay attention. The female of the breed is somewhat more responsive to training.

When he completes his course, limit his off-leash freedom to an area that is completely enclosed.

BASSET HOUND

The sad face and drooping body of the Basset Hound have become familiar to millions of viewers of TV commercials. Do not let his melancholy bearing deceive you. The upward tilt of his tail is the clue to his warm and affectionate nature.

He adapts readily to city life. He is easygoing to the point of lethargy and is perfectly content to remain alone in an apartment. The only problem the city owner will encounter is housebreaking. It takes all the energy the Basset Hound can muster to concentrate on his training.

194

Country life suits him splendidly. He behaves like a gentleman indoors and out in the yard. Although he is not physically active, he adores children and happily submits to their roughhouse play.

Off-Leash Training
Two competing forces are at work in his training. On one hand, you will have no trouble holding his attention. He is not easily distracted and has no desire to run away. On the other hand, neither does he have much desire to work.

Keep his training sessions short. Several minutes of concentrated effort on his part will exhaust him.

Be patient with him and do not set unrealistic goals. When you call him to come, do not expect him to come charging toward you. More than likely he will head your way in slow-motion time. Give him lots of praise. It is the only way you will get him to work.

Once he is trained, you may give him considerable freedom in both city and country. He is not likely to wander off.

BEAGLE

This merry little dog is a bundle of energy and activity. He thrives in an environment that gives him lots of space in which to move, to jump, and to run.

He does not make a good city dog. If he is confined to an apartment all day, he is apt to wreak havoc. This breed is known to be particularly fond of chewing carpets and couches. The key to living successfully with a Beagle in the city is to remain at home with him while he is a puppy, and give him early obedience training.

Outdoor exercise is essential. If you are a working person, provide him with a vigorous workout before you leave in the morning and again when you arrive home at night. It will be helpful if someone can take him out in the middle of the day for an additional exercise period.

He fares better in the country, where he can spend his days in an enclosed backyard. But here, too, he is apt to get into mischief. He tramples the shrubs and digs holes in the ground.

He is at his best with children. The rougher they play, the better he likes it.

Off-Leash Training

The Beagle learns slowly. Keep your training sessions short and maintain a patient attitude. He has a tendency to be stubborn. If you try to push him, he may turn aggressive and snarl.

When he finally completes his training, limit his off-leash freedom to areas that are completely enclosed.

BEARDED COLLIE

Like his Collie kinsman, the Bearded Collie hails from Scotland. Apart from his full coat of hair, however, he bears little resemblance to his distant relative.

He is a canine dynamo, and does not fare well in a city environment. If he is alone in an apartment, he jumps on the sofa, rolls over on the beds, and chews on your curtains and rugs. He matures late and his housebreaking proceeds slowly.

If you live and work in the city, plan a vigorous physical workout for him before you leave in the morning and another at night. It will be helpful if someone can take him out for an additional exercise period in the middle of the day.

He gets along better in the country, where he can run and play with children and work off some of his excess energy in an enclosed backyard.

Off-Leash Training

Training the Bearded Collie takes time. He matures late and learns slowly. He'd rather race around the training area than pay attention to his lesson. You must be firm, persistent, and endlessly patient. Eventually, you will get results.

You cannot always count on him to perform. Remaining in "Down" or "Sit" is much too dull for him. At any moment he may break his training and dash out of sight. Limit his off-leash freedom to enclosed areas in a playground or park.

BEDLINGTON TERRIER

The Bedlington Terrier has the distinction of looking like a lamb. This woolly-coated dog is aloof and sedate and fares best in an environment with one or more adults.

He is definitely not a vicious dog, but he tends to be "mouthy." If there are children in the family who play roughly with him, he may react by nipping at them.

City owners face several problems. While the Bedlington prefers a quiet atmosphere, he does not like to be left alone. If he is confined indoors, he is apt to wander through the house, chewing on your rugs and jumping on your couch. He forgets his housebreaking routine.

He is better behaved in the country, where he is able to spend many hours of each day outdoors. If you do put him out in an enclosed backyard, be cer-

197

tain the fence is a high one. The Bedlington is capable of scaling a six-foot wall.

Off-Leash Training

Your biggest problem will be motivating the Bedlington to work. Use a strong hand and be consistent in your approach. He does not work because he wants to, but because he realizes he must. Once you get this reluctant scholar moving, he learns quickly and performs well.

The male tends to be a dog fighter. Limit his freedom off leash to a completely enclosed area. If other male dogs are around, do not remove his leash at all.

BELGIAN SHEEPDOG

The Belgian Sheepdog is easy to live with. He adapts well to any environment and is equally comfortable in a city apartment or a country home. He is mistrustful of strangers but extremely devoted to his family. The more children in the family for him to run and jump with, the happier he is. His housebreaking proceeds smoothly. He is alert and intelligent and quickly learns the rules of behavior he must follow in your house.

Off-Leash Training

The Belgian Sheepdog is an excellent candidate for off-leash training. He is imbued with the work ethic and will work hard to please you. He pays attention to his lessons and learns quickly. He will respond to your commands with accuracy and speed. Praise him liberally. He thrives on your approval.

BERNESE MOUNTAIN DOG

This little-known breed is good-natured and easy-going. He maintains his sunny disposition in any environment and adapts well to both city and country life. Somewhat reserved with outsiders, he showers his own family with affection. He loves to be included in children's games.

In a small apartment, he is content to curl up in a corner and think cheerful thoughts. He gives the lie to the belief that big dogs need lots of room. He takes easily to housebreaking and responds to obedience training.

Off-Leash Training

The Bernese is a good candidate for off-leash training. He will not be distracted and run away. He wants very much to please you. But bear in mind that he is somewhat lethargic and sedate. He is apt to lag behind you in the "Heel" command, and it will take him time to respond to "Come When Called."

Work slowly and keep your sessions short. Cheer him on with frequent praise. The key to training this breed successfully is constant, exuberant praise.

BICHON FRISE

The Bichon Frise is one of the newer breeds to gain admittance into the American Kennel Club. His wavy white fur and six-pound size give him the appearance of a child's stuffed toy.

He makes an ideal family pet in either a city or country environment. His manner is affectionate and his household behavior is impeccable.

If you are a working person in the city, you may safely leave him alone indoors. He will not jump on the furniture or race through the apartment. He will not bark or chew. Instead, he will curl up in the corner and wait patiently for you to return.

The Bichon Frise needs frequent elimination walks. If you live in the city, you may prefer to paper-train him instead.

Off-Leash Training

Patience is the keynote in training the Bichon Frise off leash. He matures late and learns slowly. Do not place too many demands on him. If he senses that you are displeased with him, his feelings will be hurt. Cover the steps in each command in slow, easy stages. He tries hard. Give him lots of praise.

The Bichon Frise is both sensitive and shy. Loud street noises startle him. He is apt to become frightened and run away. Once his training is complete, limit his off-leash freedom to completely enclosed areas in a playground or park.

BLOODHOUND

The Bloodhound gets top marks for tracking down lost children or trailing fugitives from the law. Despite this formidable reputation, his disposition is affectionate and warm. He adores his master and loves to jump on people and greet them with slobbering kisses.

Because he is a large dog and needs a great deal of exercise, he does not adapt easily to a small city apartment. If he is confined during the day, he may do extensive damage to the furniture. He will work off his excess energy chewing up your drapes and nibbling on your couch. He will bark a great deal.

If you live in the city, give him a vigorous physical workout at least twice a day. Exercise him in the morning and again at night. It will be helpful if someone can take him out for an additional exercise period in the middle of the day.

Obedience training should be started as soon as he arrives in your home. The earlier you train him, the better the results. He is not an avid student and he learns slowly. Be patient with him and give him lots of praise.

The Bloodhound is happier in the country, where he is able to spend his days outdoors. Be certain the outdoor area is enclosed.

Off-Leash Training

The Bloodhound is a poor student of the off-leash commands. His attention wanders easily and he learns slowly. Choose an area with as few distractions as possible. Keep your training sessions short. Be patient with him and give him lots of praise.

When he finally completes his training, limit his freedom in both city and country to enclosed areas such as a playground or park.

BORZOI

Despite his great size, the Borzoi doesn't require much living space. He settles gracefully on the floor, stretches his long-legged, slender body into a comfortable position, and remains contentedly in the same spot for hours on end. For this reason, he adapts easily to any environment.

His manner is aloof and he tends to be a one- or two-person dog. If you live alone—or with a mate—in the city, if you will settle for loyalty instead of affection, you will live very happily with this dog.

He presents no problems in the city. He is obedient, his exercise requirements are minimal, and his housebreaking proceeds smoothly.

The Borzoi adapts just as well to a country environment. But keep in mind that he would rather lie out in the sun, thinking his aristocratic thoughts, than climb into a sandbox with children.

Off-Leash Training

The Borzoi is a good candidate for off-leash training. He is not easily distracted and you will, therefore, be able to hold his attention. While he is not overly enthusiastic about his lessons, he does respond well. Use a light touch in administering corrections. The Borzoi has a slender neck.

When his training is complete, you may give him a considerable amount of freedom off leash. He is not likely to wander away.

Bouvier des Flandres

This large and powerful dog makes an ideal pet in both city and country environments. He is gentle and affectionate and is devoted to all members of his family. The more children there are to run and play with, the better he likes it.

He combines high intelligence with a willingness to learn. His housebreaking proceeds smoothly and he rates an A in household deportment.

The Bouvier is so reliable and responsive that he is frequently used as a guide dog for the blind.

The city owner must bear in mind that the Bouvier sheds copiously. His rough, wiry coat requires daily brushing.

Off-Leash Training

The Bouvier is a perfect candidate and will graduate from his off-leash training at the top of his class.

He combines all the qualities necessary to learn quickly and well. He concentrates on his lessons, is a hard worker, and is eager to please. Give him frequent praise. He thrives on your approval.

BOXER

As a puppy, the Boxer requires a great deal of attention. He is excitable, he may wet excessively, and he cannot seem to hold still. If you leave him alone in an apartment all day, you may return home to find the rooms in a state of disarray. He chews on your furniture and jumps on your beds. The key to living successfully with a Boxer in the city is to remain at home with him during his early months.

If you live in the country, keep him outdoors as much as possible in an enclosed yard or pen.

As he outgrows puppyhood, he calms down greatly. His early excitability ripens into relaxed playfulness. He matures into an affectionate companion for the entire family.

Off-Leash Training

The Boxer is quick and responsive to his training and will learn the commands with ease. But do not be lulled into a false sense of security. He is an extremely active dog with a definite mind of his own. He may, without giving you a moment's notice, break his training and run away. Do not give him the opportunity to do so. Once his training is complete, restrict his off-leash freedom in both city and country to areas that are completely enclosed.

BRIARD

This uncommon breed is frequently confused with the Giant Schnauzer. He has, however, his own distinctive qualities. His sense of hearing is extremely acute and he makes an excellent watchdog. A sober fellow, he rarely barks or gets excited. He is quietly devoted to his family.

He is something of a stay-at-home. You may safely leave him alone in your city apartment or country house. He will spend the hours curled up in the corner, reflecting on his duties as guardian of your domain.

His housebreaking proceeds smoothly and he quickly learns the standards of behavior he must follow in the house. He is a welcome pet in any environment.

Off-Leash Training

The Briard is a fine candidate for off-leash training. Although he learns slowly, he is a plugger and stays with his lessons. He pays attention and has no desire to run away. Be patient with him and praise him liberally.

Bulldog

The Bulldog may never win a beauty contest, but he ranks high on a scale of desirable qualities. Beneath his scowling, wrinkled face and his tough-muscled body is a canine that is gentle, fun loving, easygoing, and sweet. His big heart bursts with love for his family and his affection extends to other people and dogs.

He is responsive to training and quickly learns what housebreaking means. But alas, his personal habits lack refinement. He slobbers excessively as he eats and, at odd moments throughout the day, saliva drools from the corners of his mouth. At night, he sinks into a deep sleep and snores. It is important to consider these personal traits before buying a Bulldog.

In the country, putting him outdoors cuts down on the amount of drooling he does in your house. However, the Bulldog reacts badly to hot weather. He becomes lethargic and uncomfortable and can't wait to run indoors to an air-conditioned room.

Off-Leash Training

The Bulldog responds well to training. Some members of this breed, however, tend to be stubborn. If you push him too quickly or criticize him harshly, he may display an aggressive streak. Keep your training sessions short, move along at his pace, and give him frequent praise.

BULLMASTIFF

This powerful dog with the forbidding expression on his face is as gentle as a baby and has a heart that is brimming with love. He is even tempered, likes to play with children, and curls up contentedly at his master's feet. He makes a fine watchdog. He adapts with equal ease to a small city apartment or a large country home, disproving the theory that big dogs need lots of room.

He is content to stay indoors alone. The moment you walk out the door, he'll flop to the floor and fall asleep. His housebreaking proceeds smoothly and his household behavior is above reproach.

Off-Leash Training

You will need time and patience to train the Bullmastiff off leash. He is slow to understand what it is you want him to do and he is slow to carry it out. He eases himself gradually into the "Sit" and "Down" positions and he answers your call to come at a lumbering pace. Hang on to your patience and cheer him on!

CAIRN TERRIER

This small and sturdy dog makes a fine pet in both city and country environments. He is affectionate and devoted to the entire family. An active little fellow, he thrives on joining the children at play.

He loves to run and jump and, unless you stop him, will race through the house and leap on your couches and beds.

Start his obedience training as soon as he arrives in your house. He is bright and quick to learn.

Off-Leash Training

The Cairn is one of the easier Terriers to train off leash. He learns quickly and responds to the commands with agility and speed. Typical of all Terriers, however, he has a tendency to be independent and strong willed. If he sees you hesitate or display timidity, he may decide to break out of class and run off to play. Be firm with him and use a strong hand.

The Cairn is easily distracted by such small game as squirrels and rabbits. Limit his off-leash freedom to enclosed areas in parks or playgrounds.

CHESAPEAKE BAY RETRIEVER

Not too many people recognize or have heard about this member of the Retriever family. To date, breeding is selective and the result is a superior dog.

The Chesapeake Bay Retriever adapts well to both

206

city and country environments. Although he is physically powerful and rugged, his manner is easygoing and mild. He adores children.

He is alert and intelligent and housebreaks easily. His manners are impeccable. He chews only the rawhide toys you give him and he barks only to warn you of an outsider's presence.

Off-Leash Training
The Chesapeake Bay Retriever applies himself to his off-leash training and learns quickly and well. He performs the commands with alacrity and speed. However, you must bear in mind that he is a hunting dog and there is always the possibility that some exotic scent or fascinating motion may suddenly divert his attention from you. When his training is complete, limit his freedom off leash to an enclosed area in a playground or park.

CHIHUAHUA

This tiniest of all dogs hails from Mexico and comes in two varieties—short and smooth coated, or long and silky haired.

He is an intelligent and affectionate lap dog. He is also fearful and shy. Because of his size and his timidity, owners tend to carry him everywhere. He fits easily into the crook of your arm. With his mobility restricted, he becomes increasingly attached to and dependent on his owner. How much of his insecurity and nervousness is inherent in his temperament, and how much is the result of pampering, is difficult to tell.

He is a good apartment dog and is happiest with one or two adult owners. He is a fine companion for the elderly.

207

He is not, however, a good family dog—children's exuberant play startles him. Nor can you leave him safely outdoors in an enclosed country area. The noises in the road frighten him and he may easily slip through the slats in your fence.

The Chihuahua needs frequent elimination walks. You may choose to paper-train him instead.

Off-Leash Training

The Chihuahua is quick to learn and responds to "Sit" and "Down." But since he almost never leaves your side, your arm, or your lap, you will not have much use for the off-leash commands.

CHOW CHOW

The Chow Chow fares best in a living arrangement with one or two people. Fiercely loyal to his master, he is independent and is unapproachable by anyone else.

He is noted as an outstanding watchdog. In the city he is suspicious of strangers and strongly protective toward his master. In the country, he extends his protective services to his outdoor territory and is distinctly hostile to other dogs.

He is easy to housebreak and quick to learn what he may and may not do in your home. He is also tough, aggressive, and stubborn. You must exercise a firm hand with him at all times. If he senses weakness on your part, he'll toss you a disdainful look and proceed to do exactly as he pleases.

He is not the average person's dog. But if you are strong enough to cope with him, if you admire his intelligence, his beauty, and his independent nature, you will enjoy owning him.

Off-Leash Training

It is very difficult for a professional trainer to teach the Chow Chow the off-leash commands. With his deeply suspicious nature, the Chow Chow will fight the stranger every step of the way.

If you have established a position of dominance with him, if he respects your authority, and if you exercise a strong, firm hand, you will have greater success training him yourself. He is responsive and learns quickly.

Once his training is complete, you still have to cope with his independent and hardheaded personality. Limit his freedom off leash in both city and country to areas that are completely enclosed. If your male is a dog fighter, do not remove his leash in the presence of other male dogs.

COCKER SPANIEL

The most important thing about the Cocker Spaniel is his pedigree. If he comes from reliable stock, he is apt to be friendly and quick to learn, and to make a fine family pet. But due to his great popularity in this country, the Cocker Spaniel has become the victim of excessive inbreeding. Increasingly, Cockers can be nervous and aggressive.

Check with a reliable breeder and, if possible, determine the temperament of the dog's parents. A Spaniel with the right sort of ancestors will fare well in either city or country. One from the wrong side of the tracks is difficult in any environment.

If your dog tends to be nervous, do not discipline him harshly. It will turn him into an excessive wetter or a fear biter. Be patient and be prepared to spend a great deal of time training him. With proper handling, he responds well to obedience training.

The Cocker Spaniel has an abundance of energy. If he is confined to an apartment all day, he is apt to race through the rooms, chewing and jumping on the furniture.

Plan an exercise period for him twice a day, once in the morning and again at night. It will be helpful if someone can take him out in the middle of the day for an additional workout.

Off-Leash Training

The Cocker Spaniel is quick to learn but he also tends to be stubborn. Strong-arm tactics do not work with him. He may refuse to work at all or he may become aggressive. Be patient and be prepared to spend a long time training him.

When his training is complete, restrict his off-leash freedom to an enclosed park or playground area.

COLLIE

Thanks to TV's Lassie, the Collie is instantly recognized by most people. He is a handsome animal with regal bearing and he moves with style and grace. His manner is relaxed and easygoing. He makes a fine companion for the elderly and a wonderful playmate for children.

What Lassie never taught you is that the Collie tends to be a chewer. If he is confined to an apartment all day, he will help himself to your shoes and your drapes. In the country, the chewing problem is minimized if he remains outdoors for most of the day.

The key to living successfully with the Collie in the city is early obedience training. Start his lessons as soon as he arrives in your home. As a puppy, he responds well to training; when he matures, he tends to develop a stubborn streak.

He learns his housebreaking routine easily. However, grooming is a problem. His fur sheds easily and profusely and requires frequent grooming.

Off-Leash Training
The Collie is not an easy candidate for off-leash training. He is strong willed and stubborn. Be persistent in your manner and exercise a firm hand. He understands authority and bows to a superior will.

Once he buckles down to his lessons, he makes a fine student. He learns quickly and performs the commands with accuracy and speed.

DACHSHUND

The Dachshund is a welcome pet in both city and country environments. He is happy, outgoing, and even tempered. He loves to play with children and is affectionate with adults.

He is alert and responsive to training. He learns quickly the rules of behavior he must observe in the house.

Whatever difficulties you encounter with the Dachshund are due to his physical characteristics. His bladder control is weak and he needs frequent elimination walks. Since he is small, a good alternative to housebreaking in the city is paper-training.

He has a tendency to "back problems," and climbing stairs may be difficult for him. If you live in a two-story house, plan his sleeping quarters on the first floor.

Off-Leash Training
He is a good candidate for off-leash training. He pays attention and is eager to please. However, he

does respond slowly to his lessons. It takes him time to arrange his low-slung body in the proper "Sit" position. It takes him time to understand "Down" and "Stay." Be patient and give him lots of praise.

Once his training is complete, you may give him liberal freedom in both city and country. He is not likely to wander away.

DALMATIAN

The popularity of this handsome spotted "fire dog" has brought about excessive inbreeding. This has changed his personality. Traditionally noted for his easygoing disposition, he is now frequently nervous and tense.

If you want to purchase a Dalmatian puppy, check with a reliable breeder. Look carefully into the dog's bloodlines. If either his dam or his sire is hyperactive, do not buy him.

The Dalmatian with a nervous personality does not live happily in the city. Street noises make him skittish. He fares better in a quiet country atmosphere.

City owners face two additional problems. One, the Dalmatian's housebreaking proceeds slowly. Two, if he is left alone indoors, he is apt to race through the house on a chewing rampage.

Off-Leash Training

The Dalmatian combines an intelligent mind with a willingness to please. If your practice area is free of all street noises and distractions, he will learn the commands and perform them well.

Be frugal with the amount of off-leash freedom you give him. A car suddenly screeching down the block or children shouting at play may be enough to startle him and send him scurrying out of sight.

Limit his freedom to areas that are completely enclosed.

DANDIE DINMONT TERRIER

This happy-go-lucky fellow brings cheer and joy to any environment. His manner is spirited, his high tail is carried gaily, and he gives the impression that it's great to be alive. He loves children, he loves adults, and he loves his own family best of all. He adapts well to city or country living.

Such matters as housebreaking do not concern him. He tends to ignore the routine. Start his obedience training at an early age. With his live-and-let-live attitude, he may not pay attention. Use a firm hand with him. Once he understands that you are the boss, he learns quickly and well.

Off-Leash Training

The Dandie Dinmont has the strong will of the Terrier. He likes to do things his own way. "Come When Called" is the most difficult command for him to follow. It will take time and patience to train him. Use a firm, strong hand.

Be cheerful and exuberant in your praise and make the training sessions fun. It is the only way you will get him to work.

DOBERMAN PINSCHER

The personality of the Doberman Pinscher varies with the individual dog. He may be high-strung and sensitive, or he may be calm and relaxed. Breeding is the determining factor. Check with a reliable breeder and look into the dog's lineage.

Handle your Doberman gently. With proper treat-

213

ment, he adapts well to both city and country environments. He is justly renowned as a watchdog. He is affectionate and devoted to the family. And he is an ideal dog to train.

Alert and intelligent, he responds quickly and willingly to all the obedience commands. He learns the rules of housebreaking in record time.

Off-Leash Training

The Doberman is a perfect candidate for off-leash training. He is eager to please, and he pays attention and learns quickly. He combines agility in his movements with a quick, bright mind. Conduct his training with a gentle hand. Praise him lavishly.

ENGLISH SETTER

The English Setter is placid and easygoing. As he emerges from puppyhood, he becomes downright lethargic. Jogging and working up a sweat are not for him. If you suggest a hike in the park, he is apt to look down his long muzzle at you with utter disdain.

Because he is content to curl up in the corner, he is well suited to living in either city or country. His relaxed manner makes him an ideal companion for the elderly. While he isn't overly enthusiastic about joining in children's games, he never complains.

If you live in the suburbs and send him out to the backyard, do not expect him to take advantage of his freedom to race around. He is more likely to flop into a comfortable spot and rest his weary bones.

He is extremely devoted to the family. If you are planning a family trip, it is not advisable to leave this breed at a kennel. He becomes homesick and frequently refuses to eat.

He presents no obedience problem. He is not apt to

chew or jump or bark. Such activities take more energy than he is willing to expend.

Off-Leash Training

The English Setter does not have much desire to work. Start his training at an early age. The younger he is, the more energy he has. Keep his training sessions short. Several minutes of concentrated effort on his part will exhaust him.

Be patient but firm. And do not be unrealistic in your expectations. When you call him to come, do not expect him to gallop toward you. More than likely he will head your way as if trudging through deep snow. Give him lots of praise.

ENGLISH SPRINGER SPANIEL

The English Springer Spaniel rates top marks in every category. He is handsome and intelligent, and he posseses a cheerful and even-tempered disposition. He loves the entire family. He plays happily with the children and is devoted to the adults. He makes an ideal pet in both city and country environments.

While he is thoroughly relaxed and has no emotional hang-ups, he does love to chew. However, he bears no ill will when you put a stop to this habit. He responds to all obedience training and learns quickly what he may and may not do in the house. He absorbs his housebreaking lessons easily.

Off-Leash Training

The English Springer Spaniel is bright and alert and responds quickly to the off-leash commands. But do not be deceived by his fine performance. Do not lose sight of the fact that he is a hunting dog. You

215

can never be certain when some moving object or wild game will catch his attention and distract him. After he completes his training, you may give him limited freedom. Allow him off leash in an enclosed park or playground area.

Fox Terrier: Smooth

The Smooth Fox Terrier is outgoing and energetic. His exuberant good nature makes him a cheerful companion for young and old. He loves to run with children; the rougher they play, the better he likes it.

Because of his happy disposition and because he is alert and responsive to training, he is frequently used as a circus dog.

He settles down comfortably in both city and country environments. The young puppy lives life to the hilt and, as he dashes through your house, may stop to snack on a tasty morsel of drape or a pungent leg of chair. He does not concentrate on his housebreaking.

Start his obedience training early. He is intelligent and eager to please. Once he understands what he may and may not do, you can count on him to obey.

Off-Leash Training
The Smooth Fox Terrier is an ideal candidate for off-leash training. He pays attention and is eager to please. He learns quickly. Keep your tone cheerful and let him know how pleased you are.

He performs the commands with agility and speed.

Fox Terrier: Wirehaired

Except for his coat, which is stiff and wiry and requires professional trimming, the Wirehaired Fox

Terrier physically resembles his smooth-haired relative.

It is in his personality that he differs from his kinsman. The Smooth Fox Terrier is active; the Wirehaired Fox Terrier is *hyperactive.*

He never seems to sit still. He races through the house with great bursts of speed. He jumps on your chairs and beds. He is capable of chewing an incredible amount of fabric and wood. If confined to one room, he will attempt to dig his way out.

Country living presents problems too. If you put him out in a backyard, he will set to work digging deep craters in the ground.

Obedience training is the only way to live successfully with this Dennis-the-Menace dog. Start his training as soon as he arrives in your home. He is bright and alert and quickly learns what he may or may not do.

Provide him with adequate exercise. Plan a vigorous workout for him at least twice a day.

Off-Leash Training

Because of his nonstop energy, getting him to concentrate will not be easy. Be firm with him. Once he buckles down to work, he is very responsive and quick to learn. He performs the commands with accuracy and speed.

The Fox Terrier is easily distracted by other dogs or small game. When his training is complete, limit his freedom off leash to areas that are completely enclosed. Parks and playgrounds are fine.

GERMAN SHEPHERD

The German Shepherd was born with a silver spoon in his mouth. He adapts superbly to either city or country environments, and is an excellent com-

217

panion to both children and adults. He combines a quick, bright mind with a relaxed and affectionate disposition. He is easy to housebreak and a joy to train. His popularity both as a watchdog and as a Seeing Eye dog for the blind is a tribute to his versatility, reliability, and high intelligence.

He requires a considerable amount of exercise. If you live in the city, plan a vigorous workout for him in the morning and another again at night.

The German Shepherd's popularity has led to excessive inbreeding. This has resulted in an increase of examples susceptible to hip dysplasia, a congenital dislocation of the hip. Check with a reliable breeder before you purchase your puppy. If this disease appears in his bloodlines, do not buy the dog.

Once you satisfy yourself that he comes from healthy stock, you may purchase your dog with confidence. You are buying one of the best dogs there are.

Off-Leash Training

The German Shepherd is the perfect candidate for off-leash training. Whether you work in a noisy, congested atmosphere or a quiet, isolated area, he maintains his even temper and pays full attention to your commands. He absorbs his lessons quickly and performs with agility and speed.

German Shorthaired Pointer

The German Shorthaired Pointer is essentially an outdoor dog. He thrives on exercise and needs wide-open spaces to run and to work off his tremendous energy. For this reason, he does not make a good apartment dog.

If he is alone and confined all day, he may wreak

havoc. He will race through the rooms, jumping on beds and couches, knocking down lamps and pulling out garbage. He will bark a great deal.

If you live in the city, give him a good workout in the morning and again at night. It will be helpful if someone can take him out in the middle of the day for an additional exercise period.

Obedience training should be started at an early age. The sooner your puppy learns that chewing and jumping are prohibited, the better. He is quick to learn, but he tends to be stubborn. Exercise a firm hand in his training.

He is warm and loving and makes an excellent playmate for children. His powerful muscular body is ideally suited to withstand the rough and tumble of children's play. His protective instinct is strong and he makes a good guard dog.

Off-Leash Training

Because of his hunting instincts, he is not an easy candidate for off-leash training. He chases cars and bicycles and will pursue anything running down the block. Work in a quiet area, as free as possible of moving objects.

After training, limit the extent of his freedom off leash to areas that are completely enclosed; parks and playgrounds are fine.

GIANT SCHNAUZER

The Giant Schnauzer, largest of the three Schnauzer breeds, rates high marks. His heavily whiskered muzzle and his shaggy eyebrows combine with his sturdy build to produce his rugged good looks. Calm and even tempered, he adjusts easily to any environment and lives as serenely in a

219

small city apartment as in a spacious country home.

His household manners are impeccable. He responds to housebreaking and all obedience training. He is devoted to the entire family and makes a fine playmate for children. He is an alert watchdog. To cap his list of desirable traits, his black fur is short and requires little grooming.

Occasionally, as he matures, the male of this breed tends to become a little bossy. He would like to do things his own way. Use a firm hand. He is highly responsive to authority and will quickly fall into line.

Off-Leash Training

The Giant Schnauzer is an ideal candidate for off-leash training. He brings intelligence and a willingness to work to the training area. He learns quickly and performs the commands with agility and accuracy. Let him know how pleased you are.

GOLDEN RETRIEVER

This breed is an exception to the rule that hunting dogs do not fare well in the city. The Golden Retriever adapts equally well to city and suburban living. He has only one requirement: He wants to be with you. "Wherever you go, whatever you do, I want you to know I'm following you," is an apt theme song for this breed.

He loves family life. He relishes a romp with the children and, with equal contentment, will sit quietly at your feet.

His disposition is gentle and calm. He is extremely intelligent and highly responsive to obedience training. He makes an ideal pet in either a city or country atmosphere.

A word of caution to country owners. Do not send your Golden Retriever into the backyard alone and assume he will be happy out there. He would much rather remain indoors with you.

Off-Leash Training

The Golden Retriever takes extremely well to off-leash training. He pays attention and he aims to please. He learns all the commands easily and well.

Bear in mind, however, that he is a hunting dog. Occasionally, his nose may get him into trouble. Lured by some tantalizing scent, he may follow its trail and wander out of sight. Later, he will suddenly look up and wonder where he is. He really never meant to leave your side.

GORDON SETTER

The Gordon Setter is gentle, affectionate, and loyal. He makes an ideal family companion. He is also a very active dog and requires a great deal of exercise. For this reason, he does not fare well if confined to an apartment all day. His pent-up energy may set him off on a chewing or jumping rampage.

If you live in the city, provide him with an ample workout in the morning and again at night. It will be helpful if someone can take him out for an additional exercise period in the middle of the day.

The Gordon Setter fares better in the suburbs, where he is free to romp in an enclosed backyard. Suburban owners, however, run into other problems. The dog's keen nose and hunting instinct may set him digging in the yard or attempting to jump over the fence.

The key to solving these problems is early obedience training. If you wait until he matures, these problems will be harder to cure. Exercise a firm hand in his training.

Off-Leash Training

The Gordon Setter is extremely intelligent and capable of learning all the off-leash commands. However, he is a hunting dog and is, therefore, easily distracted. Work with him in a quiet area. Without distractions, he learns quickly.

When his training is complete, give him limited freedom off leash. You may remove his leash in an enclosed park or playground area.

GREAT DANE

Despite his enormous size, it is perfectly all right to keep a Great Dane in the city. He is easygoing and somewhat lethargic and he has no burning desire to be up and moving about. He is as comfortable in a small apartment as in a large spacious house, disproving the theory that big dogs need lots of space.

He is friendly and gentle. Unaware of his own size and strength, he loves to snuggle up and lean against the members of his family. He also loves to jump on your couches and beds.

Start his housebreaking early, but wait until he is four or five months old to begin his obedience training. He matures late and learns slowly.

Occasionally, the Great Dane develops water in the joints. Hard floors will irritate him. Put a soft blanket or rug in his sleeping area.

Off-Leash Training

Because of his lethargic nature, he learns commands slowly. He is apt to lag behind in the "Heel" command and it takes him time to respond to "Come When Called." But he wants to please you and he plugs away at his lessons. Keep your training sessions short and frequent. Be patient and give him lots of praise.

GREAT PYRENEES

The Great Pyrenees is another example of a big dog that adapts very well to life in a small apartment. He is carefree and even tempered and he relaxes completely in a small amount of space.

He adores children and loves to be included in their roughhouse games. He makes a fine watchdog.

If you are fastidious about your house or apartment, there are two factors to bear in mind. First, his thick white coat sheds copiously and needs frequent brushing. Second, he slobbers all over the furniture as he wanders through the house. These factors may be less of a problem in the country, where he is able to stay outdoors most of the day.

Off-Leash Training

Training the Great Pyrenees off leash will not be easy. He is lethargic and slow to learn. He will fight you every step of the way. It is important that you maintain the upper hand and let him know who is boss. He will not work because he wants to, but because he must. Be prepared to spend a long time in his training.

After he completes his course, do not place too much trust in him. He has a habit of tuning out your commands and continuing on his own merry way. Limit his freedom off leash in both city and country to an enclosed area in a playground or park.

223

GREYHOUND

This long-legged and regal animal has the distinction of being the fastest dog in the world. He is also sensitive and high-strung.

Street noises in the city petrify him. The boisterous games of children unnerve him. He fares best in a quiet environment living with one or two adults.

If you live in the city, you need not hesitate to leave him alone in your apartment. His household manners are impeccable. He prefers solitude and the sedentary life. Walk him during the quiet hours of the day. Choose an area as free of traffic as possible.

In the country, he is happy outdoors in a secluded backyard. If the surrounding area becomes noisy, if too many children come out to play or too many cars careen down the road, bring him indoors.

Off-Leash Training

The most important factor in his training is the area you select. If it is noisy, he will become skittish and unable to concentrate. If it is quiet, he will respond well. He learns his lessons quickly and performs the commands with alacrity and speed. Treat him gently and praise him warmly.

When his training is complete, limit his freedom to areas that are both quiet and completely enclosed.

IRISH SETTER

The Irish Setter is a very active dog and requires a maximum amount of exercise. For this reason, he does not make a good city dog. Alone in an apartment, he is apt to tear through the rooms like a cyclone. He will chew the curtains, gnaw his way through a wooden chair, and, for added effect, deposit a mess on the kitchen floor.

If you live in the city, plan a vigorous workout for him in the morning and again at night. It will be helpful if someone can take him out in the middle of the day for an additional exercise period.

He fares better in the suburbs, but even there, problems arise. He is easily distracted by noises and, if he is out in the yard, will bark or attempt to jump over the fence.

He has an affectionate disposition. He adores children and loves being with the family. He also demands a great deal of attention. Do not expect to sit quietly in your chair reading the newspaper and sipping a beer. He'll bark or play the clown to get you to notice him.

His eating habits are very sloppy. He grabs the food from his dish and runs through the house with it. He slops water all over the floor.

To overcome these problems you must start obedience training as soon as you get him. Be firm with him and do not allow any infractions to go uncorrected. Once he understands that you are boss, he responds well to training.

Off-Leash Training

This intelligent dog learns easily and performs well. However, you cannot count on him to honor his training. He has an independent attitude and a tendency to wander. He moves with lightning speed and, without a leash, may wind up many miles from home. Restrict his freedom off leash in both city and country to an enclosed area such as a playground or park.

Irish Wolfhound

The size of the Irish Wolfhound is frequently enough to make strangers back away. He is the tallest and one of the most powerful of all dogs. What these strangers do not know is that beneath his formidable exterior beats a heart that is brimming with love.

He is gentle, easygoing, and affectionate. He is a welcome companion in both city and country environments.

He is on the lethargic side and devotes a good part of each day to sleep. If the doorbell rings, he will alert you with one obligatory bark and then return to his recumbent position.

You may safely leave him alone in an apartment. He is not apt to chew or jump or indulge in any other obedience problems. He may, however, quite inadvertently knock over the contents of your cocktail table with one sweep of his powerful upcurved tail.

Off-Leash Training

The Irish Wolfhound responds well, if somewhat slowly, to off-leash training. He is not easily distracted and he works to please you. But do not expect too much. When you call him to come, he is not apt to barrel toward you. More likely, he will lope along in slow-motion time. Cheer him on with praise.

ITALIAN GREYHOUND

This fine-boned and graceful dog is a miniature version of the Greyhound. He is intelligent and responsive to training.

His temperament seems to depend on his environment. If he shares his living quarters with one or two adults in a quiet atmosphere, he matures into a calm and gentle-mannered dog. But he is not constitutionally suited to deal with noise. In the country, children's exuberant play startles him, and barking dogs make him skittish. In the city, he becomes nervous and hyperactive on noisy streets.

If you live on a busy city street, walk him during the quieter hours of the day. Because of his size, you may choose paper-training instead of house-breaking.

Off-Leash Training

The Italian Greyhound is quick to learn the off-leash commands. Choose a quiet area, free of all distractions, in which to work. Make your corrections gently—he is sensitive to harsh criticism.

When his training is complete, limit his freedom to areas that are quiet and enclosed. As well trained as he is, a sudden noise may panic him into running away.

JAPANESE SPANIEL

The Japanese Spaniel proves the adage that good things come in small packages. This seven-pound beauty combines a regal carriage with an affectionate and outgoing disposition.

He adapts easily to both city and country environments. His manners are impeccable. He is much too well bred to chew on your carpet or jump on your couch. He barks only to give warning.

Despite his size, he is physically tough. He adores playing with children and thrives on their rough-house games. His devotion extends to the entire family and he makes a fine pet for the elderly.

The Japanese Spaniel requires frequent elimination walks. If you live in the city, you may choose to paper-train him instead.

227

Off-Leash Training

The Japanese Spaniel is a fine candidate for off-leash training. His body is agile and his mind is alert. He is extremely eager to please. This determined little fellow pays attention to his lessons and performs the commands with agility and speed. Give him frequent praise.

KEESHOND

The Keeshond, the national dog of Holland, is one of the lesser-known breeds in the United States. He is a furry bundle of desirable traits. Intensely devoted and affectionate, he follows you wherever you go. He trots after you from room to room and he settles happily into a sedentary position at your feet. He adores children and thrives on running and jumping alongside them. He makes an ideal companion for young and old.

His temperament is relaxed and easygoing and he adjusts with equal ease to city or country environments. Although he is not happy about being alone in an apartment, he is well mannered and trustworthy. He will settle into a corner and count the minutes until you return.

His housebreaking proceeds smoothly and he is an apt student of obedience training. He learns quickly the code of behavior he must follow in your house.

Off-Leash Training

The Keeshond is one of the better candidates for off-leash training. He is alert and intelligent and eager to please. He is not affected by noises or other distractions outside his training area. He gives his full attention to you.

He learns the commands and performs them with

228

agility and speed. The one he loves best of all is "Come When Called." He sprints across the ground to land at your feet. He likes nothing better than sitting beside you and hearing your praise.

KERRY BLUE TERRIER

This blue-black beauty is Ireland's favorite dog. Strong and sturdy, he makes a fine guard dog. He is independent and plucky and has a definite mind of his own.

If you are a working person in the city, this is not a good dog to own. He does not like to be confined indoors. He will race through the apartment, jumping on furniture and chewing up rugs. He fares better in the country, where he has some measure of freedom in an enclosed backyard.

The only way to live successfully with this strong-willed animal is to start his obedience training early and deliver it with a forceful hand. He requires an owner who is firm and consistent at all times. If he senses timidity or hesitation on your part, he will take advantage of it. The more authority you display, the more obedient he becomes.

If you admire this breed but do not trust your ability to handle him, buy a female. She makes a more tractable pet.

Off-Leash Training
Prepare yourself for a constant battle of wits. He will challenge you every step of the way. Maintain a firm posture. The stronger you are, the more successful he will be.

Once he learns the commands, you cannot count on him to honor his training. Restrict his off-leash freedom to areas that are completely enclosed. Frequently, the male of this breed is a dog fighter. If other male dogs are around, do not remove your dog's leash.

KOMONDOR

Shaggy white fur covers the Komondor from nose to tail. He resembles a big, lovable teddy bear, but, alas, he does not have a personality to match. He is strong willed and stubborn. He can be aggressive and quick to bite.

If he is left alone indoors, he chews on furniture and jumps on beds.

The Komondor needs a strong master. The key to living successfully with this breed, in either a city or country environment, is firm and consistent control. If he senses timidity on your part, he is prepared to take full advantage of you. Start his obedience training early, exercise a strong hand, and do not allow any infractions to go uncorrected. He respects authority and bows to a superior will.

He enjoys children and makes a fine watchdog. With a strong master to control him, the Komondor makes a loyal and intelligent pet.

Off-Leash Training

The Komondor is a tough candidate for off-leash training. Although he learns quickly, he is not willing to work. He will fight you every step of the way. As in his basic training, you must be firm, consistent, and strong.

Limit his freedom off leash in both city and country to a completely enclosed area in a playground or park.

The male of this breed tends to be a dog fighter. If there are other male dogs in the area, do not remove your dog's leash.

230

LABRADOR RETRIEVER

The Labrador is the most popular member of the Retriever group. He thoroughly enjoys family life and adapts readily to both city and country environments.

This dog does not know his own strength. His body is sturdy and muscular and when he rushes to greet you he may very well knock you down. The swishing of his powerful tail may send an ashtray hurtling to the floor. He is extremely energetic and loves to run and jump throughout the house. He is not recommended for elderly people.

When it comes to obedience training, the Labrador is teacher's pet. He is extremely intelligent, and he learns quickly. He is frequently used as a Seeing Eye dog for the blind.

Housebreaking is no problem and he is generally obedient. However, he does require a tremendous amount of exercise. If he is alone and confined to an apartment all day, he may become frustrated and turn to chewing. If you live in the city, give your dog a good workout in the morning and again at night. It will be helpful if someone can take the dog out in the middle of the day for an additional exercise period.

Off-Leash Training

Because of his extreme intelligence and his desire to please, he learns the off-leash commands easily. However, bear in mind that he is a hunting dog and is easily distracted. As much as he would like to oblige you, the sight or scent of a nearby squirrel is enough to take his mind off lessons. Exercise a firm hand throughout his training.

Once he learns the commands, limit his freedom off leash to enclosed areas such as playgrounds or parks.

231

Lhasa Apso

The Lhasa Apso is extremely sensitive to his treatment by the family. He basks in your love and approval. In response, he is warm and affectionate.

But he does not take kindly to criticism or punishment. If you get tough with him, he will sulk, or he may snarl or growl. And there have been times when this diminutive beauty has turned aggressive and bitten his master.

The key to living successfully with this breed is gentle handling. Treated with kindness, he maintains a sunny and even-tempered disposition and adapts well to both city and country environments.

He needs frequent elimination walks. In the city, you may choose to paper-train him. In the country, if you have an enclosed outdoor area, housebreaking works out well.

The country owner, however, faces a more extensive grooming problem. The Lhasa's long coat frequently tangles in the bushes or becomes matted if long hours are spent outdoors. Be gentle when you brush him—he will not tolerate any pulling or pain.

Off-Leash Training

The Lhasa Apso is very responsive to training. He is quick in his movements and quick to understand what it is you want him to do. He enjoys learning and performs well. Keep your tone soothing and gentle and give him lots of praise. Your approval and affection will make him want to work.

Maltese

In any contest for most desirable, all-round Toy dog, the Maltese stands the best chance to win. He combines beauty, personality, and brains. Despite his delicate looks, he is sturdy, active, and alert. His manner is sprightly and affectionate and he makes a welcome pet in both city and country environments.

Like all Toy breeds, he needs frequent elimination walks. In the country, you may send him out to an enclosed backyard. In the city, you may prefer to paper-train him.

His long silky coat requires extensive grooming.

The Maltese becomes what his owner wants him to be. If you want a lap dog, if you hold and cuddle him constantly, he will happily play the pampered darling. In this role he lavishes affection and lives contentedly with one or two adults. He resents the children getting any attention.

If you choose to give him more independence, he matures into a reliable family pet. He is highly responsive to obedience training and learns quickly the code of behavior he must follow in your house. The children become his playmates and friends.

Off-Leash Training

The Maltese is a fine candidate for off-leash training. Despite his powder-puff looks, his stamina is high and his body is sturdy. He is bright and alert and eager to please.

MANCHESTER TERRIER

The Manchester Terrier combines qualities that make him a favorite for young and old. He is quick and active and relishes vigorous play with children. He is also warm and affectionate and loves to be petted and to sit in your lap.

It is easy to keep and care for this pet in either a city or country environment. His sleek black coat

233

sheds minimally. His exercise requirements are small. He learns quickly what he may and may not do in your house.

His housebreaking, however, proceeds slowly. Start his training early and praise him frequently. He thrives on your love and goodwill.

Off-Leash Training

Training will proceed slowly but the results will prove worthwhile. Exercise patience and firmness and praise him frequently. The easiest command for him to learn will be the off-leash "Heel." This loving little animal wants to be near you and doesn't have to be told to stay close to your side.

MASTIFF

The Mastiff has the distinction of being the heaviest breed. Despite his powerful frame—he weighs as much as 185 pounds—and his formidable dark-shadowed face, he is gentle, good-natured, and calm. He is devoted to the entire family and loves to be included in children's games.

This enormous animal makes himself comfortable in small living quarters. He is easygoing and docile and, if left alone for long periods, will settle into a corner and sleep. He disproves the theory that big dogs need lots of space. He adapts equally well to a city or country environment, and you will have no trouble housebreaking him.

Off-Leash Training

With sufficient patience, you can successfully teach the Mastiff the off-leash commands. He learns slowly but is a willing worker and wants to please. He pays attention to his lessons and, as long as he hears your praise, he will continue to plug away.

234

Do not expect too much. He will answer your call to "Come," but slowly. Cheer him on!

MINIATURE PINSCHER

A diminutive version of the Doberman Pinscher, the Miniature Pinscher is a trim package of dignity and poise. He adapts well to a small city apartment. Preferring a quiet atmosphere, he fares best with one or two adults, and he is not enthusiastic about children. They're much too noisy for him.

This glossy-coated fellow is intelligent and alert and very responsive to obedience training. His housebreaking proceeds smoothly and he learns quickly the standards of behavior he must observe in your house. Fiercely protective of his small family, he makes a fine watchdog.

Off-Leash Training

The Miniature Pinscher is so attached to his master that chances are he will not wander from your side. If you choose to train him, however, he will learn quickly and well.

He is alert and intelligent and he wants very much to please. He has lots of stamina for a little fellow and will pay attention throughout his training session.

He is, however, easily upset by noise. Be certain you practice in a quiet area. Limit his off-leash freedom to enclosed areas in a playground or park.

MINIATURE SCHNAUZER

This fifteen-pound dog is a small edition of the Standard and Giant Schnauzers. He possesses their bristling eyebrows and whiskered muzzle, their compact and sturdy frame, and their overall rugged good looks.

He is a welcome pet in both city and country environments. He is playful with children and affectionate with adults. He adapts with equal ease to a small apartment or a spacious country home.

If you leave him alone in your apartment for long stretches throughout the day, you can feel confident that he will behave like a gentleman. His disposition is both independent and relaxed. He will settle into some comfortable corner and wait serenely for you to arrive home.

He learns the rudiments of housebreaking quickly. His protective instincts are strong and he makes a fine watchdog.

Off-Leash Training

You will have tremendous success with this breed. He gives you his full attention and is eager to please. He is alert and learns quickly. Once he masters the commands, he performs them with agility and speed. Reward him with exuberant praise.

NEWFOUNDLAND

The Newfoundland is as gentle and good-natured as he is powerful and strong. He lavishes affection on the entire family. He relishes spurts of vigorous play with children and is equally content to sit quietly by your side.

Staying alone in small living quarters doesn't faze him. He finds a comfortable corner and curls up to sleep. He adapts well to both city and country environments.

He is extremely obedient, and his housebreaking proceeds smoothly. However, he does have an

Achilles' heel: His table manners lack elegance. He drags his food across the floor and slobbers while he eats.

If you live in the country, you may plan to have him dine alfresco. His heavy dense coat enables him to remain outdoors in all kinds of weather. In the city, select a quiet area on a washable floor for his feeding bowl. Be gentle and give him lots of praise.

Off-Leash Training

The Newfoundland is a good candidate for off-leash training. He pays attention and wants to please. Bear in mind that he is somewhat lethargic and will tire easily. Do not push him beyond his capacities. Keep your training sessions short and be gentle in your corrections. He is extremely sensitive to your displeasure.

NORWEGIAN ELKHOUND

This robust little fellow is constantly on the move. He is quick and active and always ready for play.

He does not like staying alone. This creates several problems for the working person in the city. If a Norwegian Elkhound is confined indoors all day, he may work off his excess energy by barreling through the apartment, chewing on tables and knocking down lamps. He will bark a great deal.

It is important to give him a vigorous workout before you leave in the morning and again when you arrive home at night. It will be helpful if someone can take him out for an additional exercise period in the middle of the day.

He learns his housebreaking routine quickly. He is alert and intelligent and responds well to training.

He adjusts well to a country environment. He

loves to romp with children and he loves being outdoors. If you put him out in an enclosed backyard, make certain the fence is high. The Norwegian Elkhound is a master of the high jump.

Off-Leash Training

The Norwegian Elkhound is a good candidate for training. He has a tendency to be stubborn, so you must exercise a firm hand. The stronger you are, the more obedient he will be. When he pays attention, he learns the commands quickly and performs them with accuracy and speed.

NORWICH TERRIER

The Norwich Terrier is a bundle of energy in a small, sturdy frame. He dashes about on his short, powerful legs and seems to be saying, "It's great to be alive!"

His disposition is exuberant and loving and he endears himself to young and old. With his happy, optimistic nature, he adjusts agreeably to life in either a city or country atmosphere.

He learns his housebreaking routine slowly. Be patient with him and give him lots of praise. He will work to please you. He wants you to be as happy as he is.

Off-Leash Training

Training will proceed slowly but the results will prove worthwhile. Like all Terriers, he has an independent streak. He'd rather move along on his own merry way than remain confined in class. Be firm with him, but use a happy tone. If he is convinced that training will be fun, he will buckle down to work.

238

When he learns the commands, he performs them with agility and speed. Give him joyous praise.

OLD ENGLISH SHEEPDOG

The tremendous rise in popularity of this shaggy dog has led to excessive and indiscriminate inbreeding. The result, frequently, is a dog with a nervous and aggressive temperment.

If you are a working person in the city, you will face several problems. The Old English Sheepdog does not like to be left alone. If he is confined indoors, he is apt to tear through the rooms, chewing everything in his path. He has frequent housebreaking lapses.

His exercise requirements are high. Give him a vigorous workout before you leave in the morning and again when you arrive home at night. It will be helpful if someone can take him out for an additional exercise period in the middle of the day.

He adjusts well to a country environment, where he is able to spend his days outdoors. Caution children to treat him gently. Otherwise, he may start to snap and bite.

The Sheepdog sheds profusely and requires daily brushing.

Off-Leash Training

Training the Old English Sheepdog is difficult. He is stubborn and will test you constantly. If you are not firm with him, he will take advantage of you and ignore the lessons. Be persistent and exercise a strong hand.

The male of this breed tends to be a wanderer. You cannot count on him to respond to your commands. Limit his off-leash freedom to areas that are completely enclosed, such as playgrounds and parks.

Papillon

The Papillon has a long and honorable history as a lap dog to French royalty. He was the favorite of Madame de Pompadour. His role today is essentially the same.

It does not matter whether you live in the city or the country. If you are seeking a dog to pamper and cuddle, if you want a dog to sit in your lap and gaze at you with adoring eyes, the Papillon may be the pet for you. He is not good with children but is outstanding with elderly people.

His household manners are impeccable. He does not jump on furniture or chew. He barks only when necessary. Like all Toy breeds, however, he needs frequent elimination walks. If you live in the city, it is best to paper-train him.

City noises startle him. Cars careening down the block make him tremble. Avoid taking him outdoors when traffic is heavy.

He responds well to obedience training. If it is necessary to correct him, do so in a gentle tone. Do not raise your voice to scold him. It will make him nervous.

Off-Leash Training

The Papillon is not a good candidate for off-leash training. He is too delicate and fearful of noises. Since he spends most of his time sitting in your lap or cuddled in the crook of your arm, there is really no need.

Pekingese

Despite his small size, the Pekingese is robust, fearless, and bold. He moves with self-assurance and spunk in both city and country environments.

240

He is almost always treated as a lap dog. Owners carry him everywhere and seldom bother to train him. The result is a pampered pet. Then, if he is suddenly scolded for some misbehavior, he is apt to snap and bark. With time, his personality turns peevish and grumpy.

To bring out the best in your Pekingese, give him early obedience training. You may cuddle him all you want, as long as you teach him what he may and may not do in your house. Do not allow him to beg from the table "just this once." Correct him consistently. Be firm and gentle in your approach. The Pekingese is bright and responds quickly to training.

Like all Toy dogs, he needs frequent elimination walks. In the city, you may choose to paper-train him instead.

His tousled coat requires daily brushing.

Off-Leash Training

The Pekingese is responsive to training and is quick to learn. His stamina is high and he concentrates on his lessons. However, if his role is that of lap dog, chances are he is not going to leave your side. Training is unnecessary.

POMERANIAN

The Pomeranian is proof of the adage that good things come in small packages. He combines a happy, outgoing temperament with a quick and lively intelligence. Beneath his lush-coated beauty beats a heart filled with affection for all. He saves his devotion for his family, but he looks with warmth and friendliness on other people and other dogs. He adores children. Despite his small size, he has the stamina to enjoy their vigorous play.

241

He adapts easily to big or small families, in any city or country environment.

This sturdy little fellow is extremely responsive to obedience training. He quickly learns what he may and may not do in your house. As with all small breeds, he needs frequent elimination walks. In the country, you may conveniently send him out to an enclosed backyard. In the city, you may prefer to paper-train him.

Off-Leash Training

He is a fine candidate for off-leash training. Noises do not distract him and he pays close attention to his lessons. He is eager to please and quick to learn. When you call him to come, he will run to you as fast as his four little legs can carry him.

POODLE (STANDARD AND MINIATURE)

The Poodle, the most popular breed in the United States, is a dog that has everything. He ranks high in intelligence and is an outstanding scholar in the training class. He is playful with children, gentle and devoted to the elderly, and warm and loving to all. He is good-natured, happy-go-lucky, and eager to please. In sum, this high-fashion beauty makes an exceptional pet in either a city or country environment.

He learns his housebreaking routine easily. He does not bark excessively or chew. To cap his list of attributes, the Poodle's thick, curly hair doesn't shed. If any member of your family is prone to allergies, this is the breed to own.

Some owners tend to coddle their Poodle and not take his training seriously. The result can be a pampered and poorly trained dog. The problem is not with the Poodle; the fault lies strictly with the owner.

Off-Leash Training

The Poodle rates rave reviews in off-leash training. He brings to the training class his quick intelligence and his eagerness to please. He learns quickly what you want him to do, and he does it with precision, dexterity, and grace.

PUG

Beneath this little fellow's scowling face and sturdy, thickset body is a canine that is gentle, affectionate, good-natured, and serene. His little heart thumps with love for his family and his affection extends to other people and other dogs.

He adapts easily to both city and country environments. He loves to please and he loves to work. These qualities make him an apt pupil in obedience training. His housebreaking proceeds smoothly and he learns quickly the standards of behavior he must obey in the house.

His only problem is a physical one: He suffers from shortness of breath. Do not allow him to race around with children for any extended period of time; he will start to huff and puff long before they do. Do not leave him alone in a car on a hot day with the windows closed; he will have difficulty breathing.

Off-Leash Training

The Pug is a fine candidate for off-leash training. He pays attention to his lessons. With his gentle good nature, he performs the commands repeatedly until he gets them right. Caution: When he comes to you from a long distance, give him ample time to rest and catch his breath.

RHODESIAN RIDGEBACK

The key to living successfully with the Rhodesian Ridgeback in either city or country is firm control by a strong master.

The Rhodesian Ridgeback is a sturdy and powerful dog. He is also stubborn and strong willed. He'd rather give orders than take them. He is smart enough, however, to know when he is outranked, and he responds to a strong master.

He is not a good pet for elderly people, nor is he a good companion for a timid owner. People who are not physically strong frequently have difficulty controlling him.

He is intelligent and learns his housebreaking routine easily. He is also highly energetic and loves to jump. He jumps on furniture and on people who enter the house.

He throws himself wholeheartedly into children's games and, frequently, toddlers are frightened away. He is a better playmate for older children.

Off-Leash Training

The Rhodesian Ridgeback is a poor candidate for off-leash training. The male of this breed is frequently a dog fighter. He is easily distracted and is apt to run off. Training will be a constant battle of wills, and will require much time and effort on your part.

If you succeed in training him, you will have to limit his freedom off leash in both city and country to an area that is completely enclosed. If other dogs are around, keep your dog on his leash!

244

ROTTWEILER

This powerful animal reserves all his warmth and affection for the members of his immediate family. Bred both as a police dog and as a watchdog, he is fiercely protective of his own family and highly suspicious and hostile toward outsiders. He is a tough dog and, as he matures, has a tendency to become aggressive.

The Rottweiler needs a strong master. He has a stubborn streak and, if he senses timidity on your part, will refuse to obey. Exercise a firm hand. He understands authority and bows to a superior will.

He fares equally well in a city or country environment. His housebreaking proceeds smoothly and he is unlikely to indulge in household misbehavior. He adores children; the rougher they play, the better he likes it.

Off-Leash Training

The Rottweiler does not come to his lessons willingly. Be persistent and firm. Once he buckles down to work, he makes a quick and apt student. He performs the commands with accuracy and speed.

The male of this breed tends to be a dog fighter. If your Rottweiler fits this category and there are other male dogs around, do not remove his leash.

ST. BERNARD

The St. Bernard combines an imposing, giant-size body with a manner that is good-natured and mild. He is loving and affectionate, plays happily with children, and is content to sit quietly by your side. He adjusts easily to either a city or country environment.

245

He has a lethargic temperament, and if you leave him alone he will flop down in his favorite spot and wait patiently for you to return. He makes a fine pet for a working person.

This well-meaning dog is a sloppy eater and he slobbers a lot. He drags his food from room to room and drools saliva from the corners of his mouth.

This presents a problem for the fastidious city housekeeper. So does his dense coat of fur, which continually sheds. In the country, he can dine alfresco and much of the drooling and shedding can take place outdoors. Do not worry about the weather. St. Bernards can withstand extreme temperatures for hours on end.

Off-Leash Training

His training will proceed at a slow but steady pace. He is a willing pupil and wants very much to please. He pays attention and tries hard. Do not be unrealistic in your demands. Be patient with him as he slowly absorbs what it is you want him to do. He may not come by leaps and bounds, but he will definitely answer your call. Cheer him on!

SALUKI

The long and slender Saluki adapts best to a peaceful environment in either a city or country area.

He is happiest living with one or two adults. He'd rather curl up in the corner at your side than plunge into children's boisterous games. He does not make a good family dog.

If you do not want exuberance from your pet, if you admire grace and dignity and independence in a dog, if you will settle for loyalty instead of affection, you can live very happily with a Saluki.

246

The Saluki is somewhat lethargic and is perfectly content to remain alone in an apartment. However, city street noises frighten him. Accustom him to the sounds gradually. He will make some adjustment but he will never be completely at ease on a bustling street.

In the country, he adapts well to a small family. He enjoys being outdoors in a secluded backyard.

Off-Leash Training

In an extremely quiet practice area you will succeed in teaching the Saluki the off-leash commands. He is not, however, a good candidate for off-leash freedom. In the city, the squeal of tires or a honking horn will startle him. In a nervous panic, he may bolt and run away. In the country he may show his true colors as a member of the Hound family and take off after small game. Limit his off-leash freedom in either the city or country to an area that is both quiet and completely enclosed.

Samoyed

The Samoyed combines a proud, graceful carriage with a disposition that is loving and warm. He is devoted to the entire family and runs eagerly to join children at play. Because he doesn't require much exercise, he adapts as readily to a small city apartment as to a spacious country area.

He is bright and alert and learns his housebreaking routine quickly. What he cannot cope with is being alone. If he spends long hours indoors by himself, he is apt to become frustrated. He will wander through the house, chewing the chairs in the living room and the drapes in the den. If it can be arranged, someone should stay at home with him during his early puppy months.

247

Start his obedience training immediately. He has a stubborn streak and, initially, will resist his lessons. But once he understands that you are boss, he buckles down and learns quickly and well.

His thick and shiny white fur sheds copiously and requires daily brushing.

Off-Leash Training

The Samoyed is a good candidate for off-leash training. He brings his stubborn streak to the training area and will, at first, try to divert you from the lessons. Be firm and exercise authority. He bows before a strong master.

When he starts to work, he learns quickly. He performs the commands with agility, grace, and speed.

SCOTTISH TERRIER

The key to living successfully with the Scottish Terrier is to give him adequate attention and time. As long as he can be with his family, he adapts well to either a city or country environment. He adores children.

If you are a working person in the city, this is not a good breed to own. Left alone, the Scotty is apt to wreak havoc in your apartment. He runs through the rooms, jumping on tables and chewing up rugs. He strews garbage over the floor.

He learns his housebreaking routine slowly. The city owner must walk him frequently.

In the country, you may send him into an enclosed backyard for his elimination needs. You will, however, encounter a problem: The Scotty likes to dig holes in the ground.

Off-Leash Training

The Scotty's training proceeds slowly and with difficulty. While he likes to be with you, he doesn't want to work. Do not push him or scold him harshly. The more severely you deal with him, the balkier he becomes. You must combine persistence and patience with a tender, loving attitude. It is the only way to encourage him to work.

SEALYHAM TERRIER

The Sealyham Terrier rates high on the scale of ideal pets. He combines an easygoing attitude with a loving disposition. He rejoices in spurts of vigorous play with children and he shows his peace and contentment when he sits by your side.

He is a welcome addition in both city and country areas. Alert and intelligent, he learns quickly the standards of behavior he must follow in the house. His housebreaking proceeds smoothly. This relaxed and obedient pet also makes a fine watchdog.

Off-Leash Training

The Sealyham Terrier is a perfect candidate for off-leash training. He pays attention and learns quickly. He performs the commands with accuracy and speed.

He is true to his Terrier breeding, however, and occasionally he shows signs of rebelliousness. It is certainly more fun for him to dash about than to hold a "Sit" or a "Down" position.

Be firm with him and lavish him with praise when he complies. He really wants to please you. The more you praise him, the harder he'll try.

249

SHETLAND SHEEPDOG

This diminutive version of the Collie has finely chiseled features, a resplendent coat of fur, and an air of dignity and grace. He ranks high in intelligence, alertness, and obedience. His manner is gentle and he thrives on your love and affection. Suspicious of strangers, he takes pride in guarding his property and the members of his family.

He adapts well to any environment and makes a fine companion in either a city or country area. All he wants is to please you and earn your love. If you scold him he is crushed.

Some dogs in this breed tend to be shy or nervous. Check his bloodlines with a qualified breeder before you select one. If your dog is timid, treat him with extra tenderness and love. Although he relishes a romp with children, he may not withstand their roughhouse play.

He housebreaks easily and he quickly learns what he may and may not do in the house. However, he is unhappy when left alone. Although he is much too gentle to go berserk and wreck your house, he may decide to soothe his jangled nerves by munching on some shoelaces or a pair of leather gloves. Early obedience training, carried out with a soft touch, is essential.

Off-Leash Training

The Sheltie is a wonderful dog to work with off leash. He is extremely intelligent, is a willing worker, and he wants very much to please. He learns his lessons quickly. Keep your tone soft and soothing. He is sensitive to criticism.

Although he responds with agility when you call him to come, you probably will not have to use this command very much. The Sheltie is one of those dogs that never wants to leave your side.

250

Shih Tzu

The Shih Tzu adapts well to either a city or country environment. He combines an aristocratic bearing with a merry, playful temperament. He adores his family and is eager to please.

If you want a pet to cuddle and pamper as a lovable lap dog, he is all too happy to play this role. He is, moreover, warm and affectionate with children and always ready to join them in play.

His household manners are above reproach. He does not jump or chew. He does not bark excessively. Like all Toy breeds, however, he needs frequent elimination walks.

In the country, you can send him out to an enclosed backyard. In the city, you may prefer to paper-train him.

Country owners should be aware that the longer the Shih Tzu spends outdoors, the faster his fur becomes soiled. His profuse woolly coat requires daily grooming.

Off-Leash Training

The Shih Tzu is a fine candidate for off-leash training. He is bright and alert and learns quickly. He pays attention and will not tire during the course of a lesson. He maintains his even temper while repeatedly practicing the commands. Once he learns them, he performs them with accuracy. His thickly plumed tail wags with delight when you praise him.

Siberian Husky

The Siberian Husky loves everybody—his family, outsiders, and other animals. He does not make a good watchdog, but he is a warm and loving family

251

pet. He is happy in any environment as long as someone stays with him.

If you live alone in the city and are out of the house all day, this is not a good breed to own. In this lonely state, he will cause chaos in your apartment. He is capable of chewing a roomful of furniture and, once he is sated, sitting back on his haunches to howl.

He makes a fine pet in the country. He adores children and he loves the outdoors. His dense coat of fur protects him from extreme heat and cold.

This people lover also loves food. He begs at the table and is not above swiping the roast from your pan.

Off-Leash Training

You will have to work hard to teach the Siberian Husky the off-leash commands. While he is alert and intelligent, his attention is apt to wander to other people or animals nearby. He is too sociable and high-spirited to stay cooped up in class. Use a strong hand. Convince him that you are boss and he will comply.

You cannot give this social butterfly too much freedom off leash. When he completes his training, limit him to areas that are completely enclosed.

SILKY TERRIER

The Silky Terrier packs a lot of spunk and energy into his small, silken-coated frame. He adores children and thoroughly enjoys their vigorous play. He adapts easily to any family in either a city or country environment.

Like all Toy breeds, he needs frequent elimination walks. In the country, you can send him out to an enclosed backyard. In the city, you may prefer to paper-train him.

For a small fellow, he is unusually active and requires ample daily exercise. If he remains alone indoors for long stretches, he is apt to wander into trouble. He will work off some of his pent-up energy by jumping on the furniture and nibbling on your shoes and socks.

Start his obedience training early. He responds quickly. Be firm in your corrections but do not scold him. He is sensitive to criticism and can turn aggressive.

Off-Leash Training

The Silky Terrier is alert and learns quickly. He performs commands with agility and speed. But despite his fine performance, he is not a good candidate for off-leash freedom. He has the stubborn streak of most Terriers and a definite mind of his own. He may or may not respond to your commands. If you become impatient and scold him, he'll run the other way. Limit his off-leash freedom in both city and country to areas that are completely enclosed.

SKYE TERRIER

The Skye Terrier is a small bundle of temperament. He is fond of children but wants no part in their roughhouse play. He is affectionate to his master but refuses to take orders. If you push him in his obedience training, he is apt to snap and growl. He is suspicious of strangers and becomes overly aggressive in performing his watchdog duties.

It takes a master of diplomatic skills to live in harmony with this sensitive and strong-willed beauty. Start his obedience training as soon as he arrives in your house. Be consistent in your demands, but use a very soft touch. Be patient and give him lots of praise.

Since the Skye Terrier doesn't take kindly to discipline, he fares better in a country environment. Out in an enclosed backyard, he is free to do as he wishes for most of the day.

Off-Leash Training

Training the Skye Terrier is a long and arduous procedure. He is independent, stubborn, and strong willed. He is not anxious to please. These hurdles can be overcome if you combine firmness, patience, and affection in exactly the right proportions.

Take each command slowly. Be patient with him but let him know that you are boss. Praise him effusively when he complies.

If you succeed in training him, limit his off-leash freedom to areas that are completely enclosed.

STAFFORDSHIRE BULL TERRIER

The Staffordshire Bull Terrier was originally bred in England for pit fighting. Over the years, breeding has changed him into a loyal family pet with a docile disposition. He makes a fine watchdog.

His background of pit fighting has left him with a highly developed mouth and an almost incessant desire to chew. For this reason he is better suited to a country environment, where he can be outdoors most of the day. Be certain you enclose your yard with a high, sturdy fence. He is a high jumper and can easily scale a six-foot wall.

He is alert and intelligent and quick to understand what he may and may not do in your house.

Off-Leash Training

The Staffordshire Bull Terrier is not an easy candidate for off-leash training. He has no desire to work and he comes reluctantly to the training class. Handle him firmly and be ready to give him strong corrections. When he settles down to his lessons, he learns quickly. He performs the commands with accuracy and speed.

STANDARD SCHNAUZER

The Standard Schnauzer is a welcome pet in both city and country environments. He combines an affectionate disposition with a quick, alert intelligence. His housebreaking proceeds smoothly.

If you live in the city you may safely leave him alone indoors. His household behavior is impeccable. He barks only to give warning. He doesn't jump on furniture or chew.

In the country, his good manners extend to the outdoors. He does not dig holes in the ground or trample the shrubs.

He loves to romp with children, but their roughhouse play can cause him to snap or bark.

Off-Leash Training

The Standard Schnauzer is a fine candidate for training. He is alert and intelligent and not apt to be distracted. However, he exhibits a stubborn streak and sometimes refuses to work. Use a firm hand. Once he understands that you are boss, he quickly falls into line. He learns easily and performs the commands with accuracy and speed. Give him lots of praise. This breed thrives on affection and approval.

TOY MANCHESTER TERRIER

This dog is a pint-size version of the Manchester Terrier. Sleek and streamlined in appearance, he is energetic, active, and alert. He adores children and thrives on joining their vigorous games. He adapts easily to life in a city or country environment.

He needs frequent elimination walks. In the country you can safely send him out to an enclosed backyard. In the city you may prefer to paper-train him.

This exuberant little fellow likes action. If he is left alone indoors he is apt to run through the house, jumping on the couch and rolling over on your bed. He yaps a great deal.

The key to living successfully with him is early obedience training. He responds well to instruction and learns quickly what he may and may not do.

Off-Leash Training

The Toy Manchester Terrier is a good candidate for off-leash training. He is alert and intelligent and is quick to learn. He pays attention and is eager to please. Once he learns the commands, he performs them with accuracy and speed. Give him frequent praise.

TOY POODLE

The Toy Poodle is a seven-pound copy of his bigger brothers, the Standard and Miniature Poodles. His intelligence is superior. He is the number-one scholar of the Toy breeds. He is extremely responsive to training and adapts easily to either a city or country environment. He loves children and is affectionate and devoted to all members of his family.

256

Because of his extreme popularity, the Toy Poodle has been excessively bred, and his personality has changed accordingly. Traditionally noted for his affection, gentleness, and easygoing good nature, he is now frequently nervous and tense. Check with a reliable breeder before you purchase your puppy.

Another common problem with this breed is the owner. Owners tend to cuddle a Toy and frequently spoil him. How much of the dog's nervous temperament is due to bad breeding and how much to pampering by his master can be difficult to tell.

Like all Toy breeds, he needs frequent elimination walks. In the country, you can send him out to an enclosed backyard. In the city, you may choose to paper-train him.

If any member of your family is prone to allergies, this is the breed to own. His thick curly hair doesn't shed.

Off-Leash Training
The Toy Poodle is absolutely great in off-leash training. He has all the essential ingredients working for him. He is exceedingly bright, he pays attention, and he aims to please. He learns the commands quickly and performs them with agility.

VIZSLA

The Hungarian Vizsla combines an affectionate and lovable disposition with a hyperactive temperament. Like other hunting breeds, he needs frequent and vigorous workouts. If he is confined to an apartment all day, he is apt to race through the rooms in great bursts of speed, knocking down lamps and vases along the way. He may go on a chewing rampage or resort to barking for hours on end.

The key to keeping your Vizsla happy in the city is

257

abundant daily exercise. If you must be out of the apartment all day, plan a vigorous workout for him before you leave in the morning and again when you arrive home at night. If possible, arrange for someone to take him out in the middle of the day.

The Vizsla fares better in the country, where he can work off some of his excess energy in an enclosed backyard. He loves children; the rougher they play, the better he likes it.

His table manners will never win approval from Emily Post. He grabs his food from his dish and races through the house with it. He frequently sloshes his water all over the floor. Start his obedience training early.

Off-Leash Training

The Vizsla is a tough candidate for off-leash training. His keen nose will ferret out all sorts of interesting scents, easily distracting him from his lessons. He will have particular difficulty with "Sit-Stay" and "Down-Stay." He can be much too absorbed in sniffing the air to remain in one position for very long.

Work with him in a quiet area with as few distractions as possible. Be patient and exercise a firm hand. When he completes the course, limit his freedom off leash to completely enclosed areas in a playground or park.

WEIMARANER

The increasing popularity of this handsome and powerful gray dog has resulted in indiscriminate breeding; he is a difficult dog to own.

258

A Weimaraner is physically powerful and tough to handle. You must be firm with him. If he senses a lack of authority in his owner, he will step right up and grab control. He would much rather give orders than take them.

Because of his sturdy physique and strong will, he is not a good dog for a timid owner. Nor is he good for elderly people. He loves children, however. The rougher they play, the better he likes it.

He needs abundant exercise. For this reason, he does not make a good city dog. If he is alone and confined all day, he may work off his pent-up energy by chewing his way through the apartment. If you are a working person, provide him with a vigorous workout before you leave in the morning and again when you arrive home at night. It will be helpful if someone can take him out in the middle of the day for an additional exercise period.

He fares better in the country, where he is free to race about in an enclosed backyard.

The Weimaraner lacks etiquette. He is a sloppy eater, he begs food from the table, and he is not above swiping the meatballs from the platter. When he is sated, he jumps on your bed to sleep.

Start his obedience training early. Exercise a firm hand. The stronger you are, the more obedient he will be.

He makes an excellent watchdog.

Off-Leash Training
Like all hunting dogs, the Weimaraner is easily distracted. His keen nose is constantly seeking out the scents in an area. Work with him in a place free of outside distractions. Once his training is complete, limit his freedom off leash to completely enclosed areas in a playground or park.

Welsh Corgi

Either representative of this breed—the low-slung Cardigan or the longer-limbed Pembroke—makes a wonderful pet in either a city or country environment. The Corgi is an industrious fellow who works very hard to please you. He concentrates on his housebreaking and quickly learns the proper schedule.

If you live in the city, you may safely leave him indoors alone. His household behavior is impeccable. He barks only to give warning. He doesn't jump on furniture or chew.

In the country, his good manners extend to the outdoors. He does not dig holes in the yard or trample shrubs.

He is an exuberant playmate for children and an affectionate companion for adults.

Off-Leash Training

The Welsh Corgi is a perfect candidate for off-leash training in city or country. Noises do not distract him. He learns quickly and he performs the commands with accuracy and speed.

Be sure to praise him. He thrives on your approval.

Welsh Terrier

This small and sturdy pet is a bundle of whirlwind activity. He expresses his joy at being alive by racing through the house in great bursts of speed. He adores children. The rougher they play, the better he likes it. He is an exuberant companion for his master.

A sedentary city life is not for him. If he is left alone indoors for long hours throughout the day, he is apt to make a mess of an apartment. He will jump on your couch and roll over on your bed. He'll chew the rugs, the baseboards, and the chairs.

If you are a working person in the city, be sure to provide him with ample exercise. Give him a vigorous workout before you leave in the morning and another when you arrive home at night. It will be helpful if someone can take him out for an additional exercise period in the middle of the day.

He fares better in a country environment, where he is able to spend most of his day outdoors. He works off his excess energy zooming around the backyard. Occasionally, he stops to dig deep holes in the ground.

In either city or country, the Welsh Terrier needs obedience training. Start his training as soon as he arrives in your home. Be firm and exercise a strong hand.

Off-Leash Training

The Welsh Terrier is a difficult candidate for off-leash training. He is much too active to stand still and pay attention. Use a strong hand and give him firm corrections.

When he settles down to work, he learns the commands easily. However, you cannot count on him to perform. When you call to him, he may or may not come. Limit his off-leash freedom in both city and country to areas that are completely enclosed.

WEST HIGHLAND WHITE TERRIER

The Westie rates top marks as a family pet in both city and country areas. This spunky little fellow is good-natured, self-confident, and relaxed.

He has an endless supply of love for every member of the family. He is gentle with the elderly, exuberant with children, and warm and loving to everybody in between.

Alert and intelligent, he learns rapidly what he may and may not do in your house. His housebreaking proceeds smoothly.

Off-Leash Training

The Westie has all the qualities to insure rapid and successful training off leash. He is attentive and bright and understands quickly what it is you want him to do. He takes great pleasure in showing you how well he performs. He executes the commands with speed and perfection and thoroughly enjoys his training. Reward him with lots of praise.

WHIPPET

The sleek and slender Whippet adapts best to a peaceful environment in either a city or country area.

He is a one- or two-person dog. He makes a fine pet for the working couple but shies away from children and their roughhouse play.

If you do not require exuberance from your pet, if you admire grace and dignity and independence in a dog, if you will settle for loyalty instead of affection, you will enjoy owning a Whippet.

He adapts very well to life in a city apartment. He prefers solitude, and his household manners are impeccable. However, the street noises in the city frighten him. Accustom him to such sounds gradually. He will make some adjustment, but he will never be completely at ease on a bustling street.

In the country, he adapts well to a small family in a peaceful atmosphere. He enjoys being outdoors in a secluded backyard.

Off-Leash Training

The Whippet is a poor candidate for off-leash training. Outdoor noises unnerve him. Although he is intelligent and responsive to training, it will be difficult for him to concentrate. Choose an area as free of noises as possible. Be patient and gentle.

If you succeed in training him, you must limit his off-leash freedom. In both city and country, select areas that are quiet and completely enclosed.

YORKSHIRE TERRIER

The Yorkie makes up in spunk and self-confidence what he lacks in size. He possesses a sturdy body and a definite mind of his own. He adores children and is tough enough to withstand their roughhouse play.

The Yorkie is happy in either a city or country environment, but, wherever he is, he lets you know he's there. He races through the house, yapping as he goes. He jumps on your beds and your couch.

He disdains your efforts to housebreak or paper-train him. He is much too excitable to pay attention to his training.

The only way to live successfully with this little fellow is early obedience training. Do not assume that because he is small, the jumping and yapping don't matter, or that he will eventually develop the proper manners. The older he gets, the more independent he becomes. Start his training as soon as he arrives in your house. Be firm and consistent in your approach.

Off-Leash Training

If you do not treat your Yorkie as a lap dog, if you have successfully trained him in obedience, he will make a fine candidate for off-leash training. He is sharp-witted and quick to understand.

Although he performs the commands easily, you cannot always count on this free-spirited creature to obey. Something may suddenly catch his attention and he will be off and running. Restrict his off-leash freedom to areas that are completely enclosed.

Index